KV-371-141

A Computer for your Church

Malcolm Dunlop

SPCK

CANCELLED
DEINIOL'S HAWARDEN LIBRARY

First published in Great Britain 1986 by
SPCK, Holy Trinity Church, Marylebone Road, London NW1 4DU

Copyright © Malcolm Dunlop 1986

All rights reserved. No part of this book may be reproduced or
transmitted in any form or by any means, electronic or
mechanical, including photocopying, recording, or by any
information storage and retrieval system, without permission in
writing from the publisher.

British Library Cataloguing in Publication Data

Dunlop, Malcolm
   A computer for your church
   1. Great Britain—Church history—1945–
   I. Title
   254.3   BR743.2

   ISBN 0-281-04222-5

Phototypeset by Tradespools Ltd, Frome, Somerset
Printed in Great Britain by Whitstable Litho Ltd, Whitstable, Kent

Contents

ACKNOWLEDGEMENTS

I acknowledge with grateful thanks the help I have received in preparing this book. In particular I should mention the time and assistance so freely given by: Mrs Fay Dain, Mr Adrian Burns, the Rev. Thomas Steel, the Rev. Stoker Wilson, and the Rev. R.A. Moore. I would also like to record my thanks to Mrs Margaret Sizer for patiently retyping the many drafts.

PRICES AND SPECIFICATIONS

While every effort has been made to confirm both prices and specifications with the sellers, no responsibility can be taken that these are current. Buyers should verify up-to-date prices and specifications when planning their purchase.

A Computer for your Church

1

Why do you need a computer?

The Church has unparalleled experience in information technology. Often it has pioneered and perfected it. Sometimes it has resisted it. Almost always it has taken it to heart in the end. The Christian Church possesses one of the most precious databases, on the relationship between God and Man, in existence. It has not hesitated to produce special-purpose buildings to communicate with the local population; to equip those churches with that versatile and highly developed musical instrument, the church organ; to encourage some of the finest early music, as well as some of the most popular music; and to invest in stained-glass windows and symbolic furniture.

The Church has always contained those who have seized on new technology. When Caxton came back from Cologne with the new movable type, the Church rushed to print Bibles. The Church has also to a greater or lesser extent adopted the magic lantern, audio-visual presentations, amplification systems, addressing machines, typewriters, and motor cars. Yet in 1985 the Anglican Bishop of Madagascar still travelled hundreds of miles a year on foot to his outlying villages. Still, today, most of the problems to do with spiritual needs remain those that pressed upon the shoulders of the early Fathers of the Church.

In the Church, therefore, we find a blend of both open-minded readiness to accept innovation, and also a down-to-earth, practical attitude to life that is essentially part of the Christian pastoral heritage. We believe that the computer offers an exciting new pastoral link between a minister and his flock.

1

Using a computer

By 1985, 1000 of the 36,000 ministers in the United Kingdom were members of the Church Computer Users Group (CCUG). Five hundred of these were Anglicans. And of the very wide range of computers used, over 400 were Sinclair 'Spectrums'.

From our own research it seems likely that there are a similar number of computer users who are not members of CCUG because either they have sufficient knowledge to handle their own computing problems, as at Holy Trinity, Brompton, where an Administrative Manager runs the computer, or the church has the loan of somebody else's computer, as at St Mary's, Beaconsfield, where a professional computer programmer in the parish kindly keeps essential church information up to date. This means that 2000 churches already use computers, or about 5%.

Why do these churches use a computer? While it is hard to capture the versatility of the computer in church life, *the two key uses are to ease the administrative burden and to extend outreach*. Every minister develops his own style of ministry and one thing is certain: the computer will adapt to his way of working. There is no need, if you use a computer, to adapt your approach.

It is perhaps worth making the point here that young people are used to computers in their homes and at school, and the opportunity therefore exists to involve them in any church computer activity. In addition, many Christian computer stories and games exist to attract the young.

Making a start

A computer is as easy to use as a word processor. Once the computer is installed in your office, you should be able to get your first letter off the same day. To compose a letter on a little television screen and get it exactly right before you print it, can be an enormous relief to a minister whose part-time secretarial assistant may only come in once a week.

Next try composing your Order of Service. You need never

lay out another again! Just modify the last one with the details of the next, retaining the layout and heading.

The next common use is to try to get your computer to sort out the details of people in the parish. By being able to list their names and addresses and also key features such as those who take the magazine, those who are on your visiting list, those who have been baptized or married or those who are on the management committee, you can get a wonderful grip of parish organization. For instance, sending a Christmas card to every person connected with the church can be a simple job of running off 600 labels over the lunch break. Parish magazines can go out to street distributors with totally up-to-date lists of names and addresses which themselves can be returned by the parish magazine distributor with notes of changes of address, changes of occupier, etc., to be fed back into the computer. Or, if you are visiting an area, the computer can remind you who lives there whom you had planned to visit, or give you a list of names of unvisited church contacts.

A computer filing system can be a valuable tool to the minister in letting him do his own work better, and a way of letting lay people fulfil responsibilities for the minister.

Managing money

A computer will also handle the records of allocating money handled by a church on behalf of the minister and others. Much work has been done in this area by the pooled experience of the Church Computer Users Group and several dioceses.

Your church may have trust funds, for which full statutory accounts must be kept. A wide range of systems is available to manage the accounts. For a particularly well-endowed church like All Souls, Langham Place, a computer is justified for this task alone. It is simpler to enter each movement of money through one keyboard operation into many different ledgers kept electronically than to keep reaching for different ledgers and sorting the entries manually. The computer will add, subtract and multiply automatically as you use it, so that running totals are always available on every set of accounts without the trouble of having to tot them up yourself.

Helping your work

Finally, a computer can help you just to be yourself. It may be important to remember what sermons you have preached, when and in which churches, which hymns you like to be associated with which themes, which hymn tunes are available to you with each organist. Any such record is easily kept. Are baptisms an important recruitment point in the church? Do you want to concentrate on the families and godparents, with follow-up cards and trial complimentary subscriptions to the parish magazine? These are a mere sample of the roles taken on by a computer in a few churches. Note too that the Inland Revenue now recognizes a computer as an essential business tool: see Appendix I.

The Rev. Stoker Wilson of Greenside has mastered twenty-one separate tasks on his computer, which are listed with his kind permission in Appendix II. To quote him:

> In the parish, the computer allows me more time to deal with people. It allows those people who help me with administrative tasks to do those tasks better. I do not find using a computer de-personalizing. It keeps bringing names in front of me. I do not know what I would do now in my ministry without a computer.

2

What is a microcomputer?

A microcomputer is simply a very small version of a huge machine used by banks, insurance companies and the like. Just as a baby is a small human, your church needs only a small computer. So when we refer to a computer, we mean the size of computer that is appropriate to your needs: a microcomputer.

What it's all about

Most people fear computers, and with good reason, because they represent a new unknown. Introducing movable type caused real worries and fears in many a pastoral heart, as has the introduction of the electric guitar into some services! Similarly, introducing a computer into a church may worry some people, but a church computer will never be as potentially lethal as the minister's car—nor need it be as controversial as introducing a new order of service.

A computer is made up of five simple, homely devices that can be equated to:

> a typewriter
> a calculator
> a TV screen
> a tape-recorder
> a filing cabinet

Have you ever been concerned at the thought of using any of these before? They correspond respectively to the keyboard and

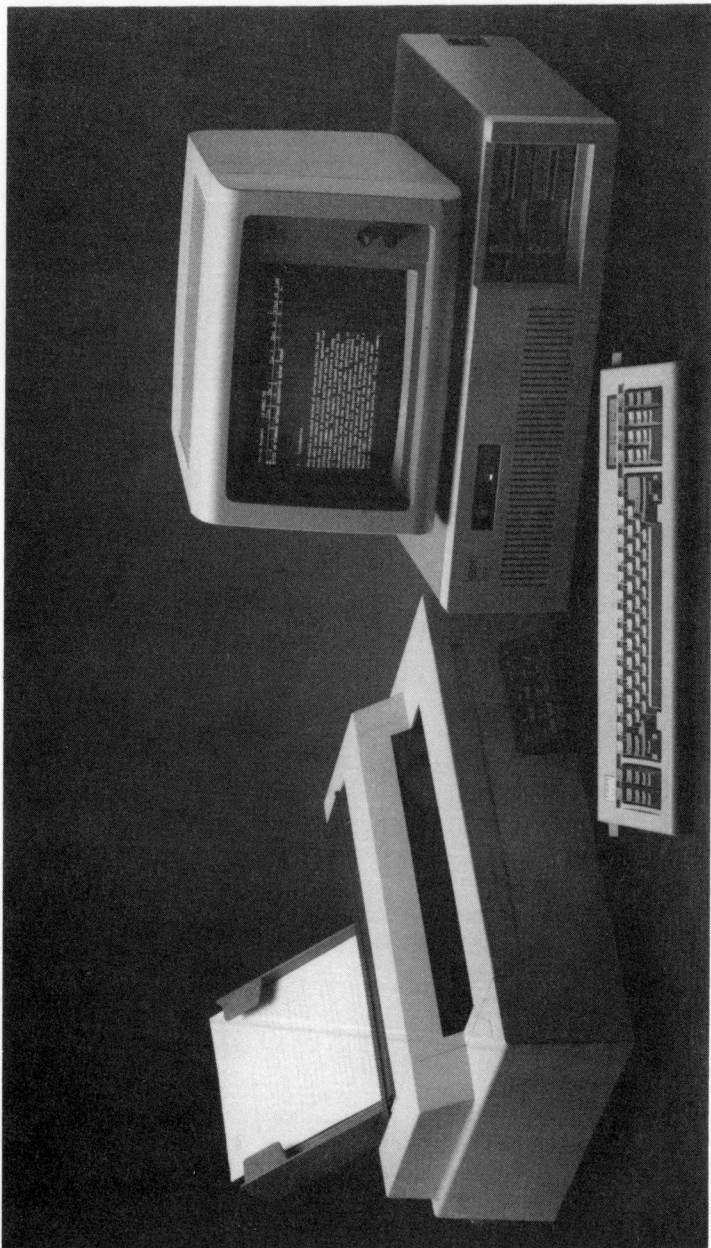

The IBM Personal Computer XT

printer; the central processor; the monitor; and, for the last two, the disk drives or tape.

'A typewriter'

If you already possess a modern, electronic typewriter you only need look inside to notice that the keys are not connected to the print-head with bars of metal, but with a flat, flexible lead. If you do not have one, ask someone you know who has an electric typewriter to let you look inside. This lead takes a signal each time you tap a key and passes it to tell the print-head to impress the character that you selected. Just as the words used to dictate this book are transient and lost unless captured on a small cassette-recorder, so the signals between the keyboard and the print-head need to be captured if they are to be processed, stored and used. Computers capture these signals in a form of magnetic storage. So you may regard a computer as a typewriter that has had the wires to the print-head cut and fed to a magnetic storage system, from whence those signals can be played back, altered or manipulated.

The screen

A computer adds a pocket calculator to the typewriter. The window in a calculator quickly reports your results and saves the reams of paper that would otherwise have to stream out of it. This window is enlarged on your computer into a TV-like screen that is able to display twenty-five rows of letters, each eighty characters (letters) long.

A memory

Calculators have memories. You can add to or subtract from, figures in the memory or read or erase it, as you wish. Your computer also has a memory, but of many thousand characters.

It enlarges the calculator's memory and screen enormously, and makes them of far greater use.

Programs

Even the meanest calculator will give you the square root of a number. This is done by telling the calculator to take a series of logical steps, just as the notes on a sheet of music tell an organist to take a series of musical steps. That these steps are recorded inside the calculator for repeated use is no more a mystery than that every note of a Beethoven symphony may be available on a high-quality cassette. We call this series of logical steps a *program*. While only a dozen or so steps are recorded in a calculator, a computer will record thousands of steps in a very complex series of events and cope with an almost infinite series of logical solutions.

Filing facts

Most pastors keep a card index to show the name, address and telephone number of members of the congregation. Those index cards could have been typed. The typescript could be intercepted and stored magnetically by computer. Once captured, each card could be projected from the computer's memory on to the screen just as numbers come up on the screen of a calculator. You can then edit that card from the keyboard as often as you wish, or print out all or part of any card on the computer's printer to use as a prompt for a follow-up visit.

Sorting facts

Any computer will uncomplainingly eat up work, unbelievably fast, on the dullest and most tiresome tasks. The calculator part will process several million electronic characters per second. It would take only a moment to look through the whole church members' list, or to print a list of ladies in the parish to be invited to a special mothers' meeting. The computer will have looked through any records you have put in to give you an alphabetical list divided, say, by streets or districts, of those ladies whose surname is prefaced by Mrs, or by age group. By the time you had taken a cup of coffee the list could be ready on adhesive labels!

Writing letters

Glancing down a list of church members, some name may strike your eye, and you subconsciously compose the words of the invitation to a meeting. Why not sit down at the typewriter keyboard and capture those words promptly on the computer? You can then examine them on the display screen, rearrange and polish them, and, on departing for lunch, ask the computer to address, by the salutation you use personally for each person, an otherwise identical letter of invitation. You return from lunch to find all copies run off, and ready for matching to the labels.

An essential business tool

There is no need to understand in detail how or why a computer works to make good use of it. Few of us really know how an electronic typewriter works, nor understand the inner workings of a pocket calculator. We use a photocopier and take on trust its optical complexities. And most of us ignore the inner workings of our car. The aim of this book is to prove both to ministers and management committees that a small computer is an essential business tool to the minister who can usefully employ it.

We will present a strong case for a computer as essential equipment for a church. You yourselves will have to settle the order of priority, juggling the demands for a replacement car, a photocopier, a new typewriter, repairs to the central heating, a telephone answering machine and all the other pressing needs for capital equipment in your church.

The remainder of this book will encourage you to understand how to use a simple business microcomputer, and explain its four main parts: the central processor, the keyboard, the screen and the printer, so that you can choose the right computer for your church.

3

The central processor: the thinking bit

'Thinking'

How on earth can a computer read and write? How can it appear almost to think? The answer lies in the fact that mathematics is merely a shorthand for logic. Almost any logical statement can be expressed mathematically. You will already be familiar with the sort of logic that computers use through the thermostat and time-switch that control a room heater. *If* a room is too cold *and* the time is right for heating, *then* the heater comes on. *If* the room warms up enough, *or if* the time for heating ends, *then* the heater turns off. The statements *if, and, then, or if,* have formed the logical steps of a very simple program. And they remain at the heart of a typical computer program, however complex.

The microprocessor

Inside every microcomputer, a little chip of silicon has been photo-etched to provide a wide array of circuits that perform these, and similar logical steps. Pulsing to a built-in clock it permits, say, five million steps to be taken every second. It is this sheer speed that allows an incredible number of dull, tediously logical steps to be taken to solve a simple problem. This is called the microprocessor chip.

At its heart the computer only recognizes two numbers, 0 and 1. We could say that a computer counts on only two fingers instead of ten: it does 'binary arithmetic'. Fortunately binary arithmetic allows these two numbers to process the whole range of known mathematics, and hence the whole field of logic. At heart, the computer is just a totally obedient automaton; it lacks all flair, intuition and insight. All it can do is follow a tortuous path of tediously repetitive *yes/no* questions until it finds a little part of an answer; it then goes back to the beginning and starts again on the next part of the answer.

The memory

All these results are stored away in another silicon chip called the random access memory (RAM). This has been photo-etched quite differently to store data at thousands of little storage points called addresses. The very cheapest home computer has probably got 2000 such addresses and the average small business computer at least 64,000.

Your computer's capacity is governed largely by its memory size. The memory must be big enough to take in the program commands to tell the microprocessor chip what to do next, and the intermediate results that come out of the processor. Never buy a home microcomputer with less than about 32,000 characters of RAM, which we call 32K. Most ministers have found they need about 48,000 characters of RAM (48K) to run the sort of business programs usually loaded from a cassette-recorder. But a church ought to consider buying a small business computer, a twin-disk machine with a RAM of 64,000 characters (64K) or 128,000 characters (128K).

Using binary arithmetic almost unbelievably fast, a microcomputer takes instructions from its memory and processes them in its processor chip to resolve any logical problem.

Some makes of microcomputer put parts of their disk operating system on a separate little silicon chip to save the precious random access memory space. To protect you from accidentally altering that chip and thereby the operating system, this is made a read only memory, or ROM for short.

A church is not likely to need extra computer memory but fortunately nearly every microcomputer has facilities to let you plug in extra memory should your initial purchase prove too small for your needs.

8 and 16 bit

The microprocessor chip is either arranged to process groups of eight binary characters at a time (enough to cover all the characters of the keyboard and to address up to 64,000 characters of memory), or the newer chips can deal with sixteen binary characters at a time (which allows a microcomputer to be built with up to four million addresses of memory storage). These computers are said to be 8-bit, or 16-bit, respectively. The microprocessor chip and its memories form the central processor unit (CPU).

Reading and writing

A computer reads and writes by allocating a code number to every single character, space and function of the typewriter keyboard. It encodes every tap of the keyboard before storing it magnetically as that code number. When it writes, the computer sends these code numbers to the screen or the printer unit which then interprets them locally back into the appropriate print commands. The code it uses to do all this is called ASCII (American Standard Code for Information Interchange) and was developed a long time ago to standardize teleprinter circuits in the United States. So this is a very well-established and reliable system of reading typewriter keys and writing messages.

You need minimum 32K RAM, preferably 48K, for a suitable home computer. You need minimum 64K RAM, preferably 128K, for a twin-disk business microcomputer.

4

The keyboard: a gentle touch

The layout

Practically all the information that ever goes into your computer will get in through the keyboard. So the quality of keyboard is important. It will also affect the price. Lots of computers such as the small Sinclairs with their rubber buttons, and the many computers with compact, sometimes stiff, keyboards that have no room for both hands to be spread across the keys, are sold to satisfy 'two-finger typists' and those who want to learn programming.

If you enlist the aid of skilled typists or book-keepers from your church they will have sensitive fingers like a pianist's and will expect their fingers to be able to fly lightly and subconsciously across the keys. So the keyboard must be laid out wide enough for their fingers to lie naturally across the keys. The keys themselves should for preference:

- be on a separate, low, platform that can be arranged conveniently for each person's typing, on a flex, not permanently fixed to the computer.

- be light to the touch and consistent. One or two keys that 'stick' will distress a good typist.

- have the keytops 'sculpted', with depressions to fit the tips of fingers.

- have the keytops spaced between rows, to protect female fingernails from breakage.

14

- have the top row of the letters reading QWERTYUIOP. Avoid keyboards that do not.

With such a keyboard, a skilled typist will enjoy helping you get your facts into the computer.

Numbers

Book-keepers will also have developed subconscious skills. Their fingers will fly over the standard '10-number' keypad instinctively. Indeed you may find that this is the first skill you acquire yourself. The 10-character keypad is so easy to use that your fingers seem to learn without conscious effort. Without a keypad, numbers have to be put in slowly via the top row of the typewriter keyboard.

If this keyboard is outside your budget a more limited keyboard, built on top of your computer, will still give you good service, as the 400 clerical users of the 'Spectrum' will witness.

'Clicks'

The better keyboard has such light keys that those who grew up with old-fashioned typewriters feel lost. For those who have learnt to associate a successful keystroke with a healthy click or bang, some makers provide an electronic 'click' each time a key is successfully depressed. Most people who use this aid find that they leave the 'click-switch' off as they gain experience and confidence.

Control keys

Typewriters use 'shift' keys to type capitals. Computers add up to three more control keys to provide the *shift, control, escape* and *alternate* keys. It is worth seeing if any keystrokes that you know you would have to make call for too much dexterity. It is annoying to have difficulties with poorly laid-out control keys.

Function keys

On the smaller computers, a control key plus a letter key pressed together will tell the computer to perform quite compli-cated tasks. To save remembering these different control/letter combinations, the better keyboards add further command keys, typically labelled F1 to F10, called *function keys*. One *function key* replaces pressing a combination of control/letter keys. *Control*, *shift* or *alternate* can modify the function keys to give in total 40 keys-worth of special command operations from the usual 10 function keys.

Function keys are either in two vertical columns at the left-hand side of the keyboard or in an extra row along the top. There seems yet to be no common consent as to which layout is better. It is probably easier to learn with the line across the top. With experience it is easier using the left little finger to operate two vertical left-hand columns.

Function-key overlays

A way to remember what each function key does is to buy a thin rubber or plastic cut-out mat or overlay which lies around the keys and says what they are used for. The better word-processing programs have overlays for the major makes of microcomputers.

Caps-lock and shift-lock indicators

The better keyboards have lamps embedded in *numbers-lock, caps-lock* buttons to show when the button is 'depressed' and active. Without these lamps it may be difficult to remember the status of that button and so accidentally make an error. This is a weakness of the IBM personal computer's numbers lock and causes some frustration.

The *caps* button is used to 'Shift' only the *letters* on the typewriter keyboard into capitals, leaving the numbers and

16

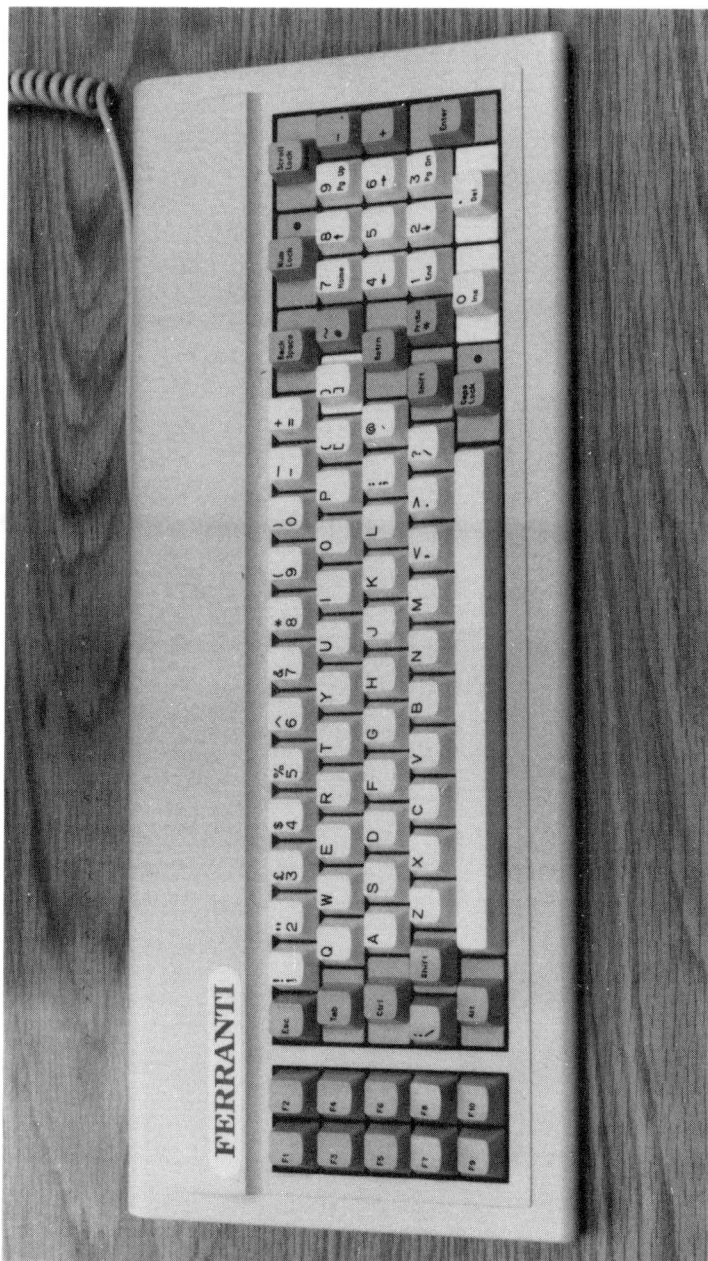

Business Grade computer keyboard

Keyboard of the Sinclair Spectrum Plus

symbols in normal lower-case. This is particularly useful for programs which recognize the difference between capitals and lower-case (small) letters. Avoid *caps-lock* buttons which also 'shift', and so lose, the numbers across the top of the QWERTY keyboard. Test before you buy.

What you need

When you are buying, think whether a skilled typist or book-keeper is ever going to feed in information. If so, keep away from the cheaper, smaller microcomputer keyboards. If you have no outside help, consider going to evening classes to save wasted hours in two-finger typing. If you are determined, however, to stay a resolute two-finger typist and restrict use to you and your like, then a simple keyboard like the 'Spectrum' or BBC will suit you. Avoid the smallest, flexible rubber, keyboards used on the earlier Sinclairs for everything except learning to program or games.

5

The screen: eye contact

The part of your computer that looks like a TV screen, the monitor, is most important. It is through the screen that the computer responds instantly to your promptings.

Size, reflections and tints

Screens are usually 9″ or 12″, measured across the diagonal of the tube. Smaller than 9″ is usually over-tiring to middle-aged eyes.

If you buy a screen with a matt surface etched on to the face glass, it reduces glare and eases the eyes. Screens with a shiny surface reflect highlights and dazzle you. Try to avoid screens where the anti-dazzle surface is stuck on to, or mounted, in front of the screen. Dust gets behind, or into, these and dims the display. They are also tedious to clean. The best matt surface should cost you no extra.

You will usually want to change the brightness, contrast, etc., as the room gets darker or brighter, so front screen controls are helpful.

Some people who find a black and white screen tires the eyes enjoy the softer contrast of a green display. A gold display has many advocates for use under fluorescent lighting. Neither of these tints should cost extra.

Dots

Each character on the computer screen is made up of dots of light arranged in columns and rows. The more dots, the clearer, neater and more solid the letter. So a character of many dots on a 9″ screen may look better than one of few dots on a larger screen. A screen offering 7 × 5 refers to a maximum number of 7 vertical dots in each of 5 columns. Do not use fewer except for programming. Try to get a 7 × 7 or 9 × 7 matrix. Anything better is a pleasant luxury.

The less your brain has to do to recognize each character, the less tiring the screen is to use. Much operator fatigue is due to tiredness of the eyes caused by poor character outlines.

Flicker

'Flicker' – a fluctuating brightness of light – on the screen causes unconscious eye-strain often associated with general fatigue and a headache. It occurs because only one jet of electrons is used to light up in turn each dot on the screen, and so there is time for that dot to fade before the jet gets round to it again. This is perceived as a very fast flicker on the surface of the screen. One way of reducing flicker is to use a phosphorescent coating on the screen that keeps on glowing. This causes a nuisance in word processing when ghost images stay behind on the screen. It is better to 'refresh' the screen by regularly firing a very weak scatter of electrons at the screen just to keep the little points of light glowing bright. The best screens do this sixty times (cycles) per second or faster. Fifty times (cycles) per second is acceptable but can get in step with the flicker of any fluorescent light.

Position

Middle-aged eyes find any screen that is physically mounted as part of a solid computer and keyboard tends to be at 'super-market-shelf distance' and hard to focus on. It is helpful to be

21

able to push the screen at least a foot back from the keyboard.

A tilt-screen adjusts according to the individual sitting positions of people with short or long backs and also helps avoid glare from windows behind the operator or overhead lights. A swivel-screen allows you to discuss the contents with a colleague without having to vacate the keyboard to let him or her see properly. It is worth buying one of these screens.

Size of display

Most home-computer screens offered are normally set to show lines of text only forty characters wide. This is bad for word processing on A4 paper as you cannot see the true layout. Although salespeople will tell you of ways round this, there is no substitute for a screen which displays lines eighty full-sized characters long. For good, practical reasons the screen should be able to display twenty-four rows at a time and preferably a twenty-fifth row. Such screens are known as '24 × 80' or '25 × 80' character screens.

Colour

Certainly colour is fun, but it costs more and uses up more computer memory to run. As you can usually organize computer games on a TV set, however, we recommend keeping any money you might have spent on a colour screen for a higher grade printer and/or keyboard. Not every computer arrives equipped to handle colour. Note that it may be costly to add colour facilities later.

For games and message boards, a colour TV set will be suitable. But TV sets compose poor letters of the alphabet that flicker in lines too short for A4 text, and are best avoided for business purposes. Many small computers will drive a TV set, but may tend to spoil it by 'scorching' the screen.

If your computer has an RGB (red, green, blue) socket to drive a TV set, it can open up a whole new field for Christian

The IBM Personal Computer XT, with colour graphics display

evangelical outreach, the Christian computer game, and the computer message board for advertising a bookstall, a special collection or event, or even asking people to pick up parish magazines at the end of the service. A message board should be easily composed by a sixteen-year-old who is doing well at computing at school. He or she may ask to be allowed to add sound effects. Provided the occasion is right, sound can add a vital dimension for games and message boards.

The cursor

On every screen there is a splash of light, an underline, or a square box, which tells you where you are, the 'cursor'. It indicates where the next letter will be printed. You can often choose its shape and also make it flash. There are usually buttons with arrows on to move the cursor around the screen independently of the typewriter keys.

What you need

You need a computer screen. The letters in twenty-four rows of eighty columns should be made up of at least 7×5 dots, preferably more. The surface should be etched to reduce reflections. The text should not flicker. The 9" Apricot screen is all right; otherwise buy a 12" screen. Colour and 'high resolution' are luxuries that you probably do not need.

6

The printer: for the record

You need a printer. A printer provides the visible results of your computing. What comes up on the screen is transient; what comes out on the printer remains to be examined at leisure or circulated or stored. If your computer is to help with the business of running the church, then you must get to know what printers will do for you, and why, *before you buy the computer*.

Most new computers come designed to drive a particular family of printers. We know of one international firm that equipped its Hong Kong office with over £150,000 worth of printer, which they then found their computer could not drive. This chapter is designed to save you from a similar mistake.

Printers come in four main types: thermal, daisywheel, matrix and ink jet.

Thermal printers

These are generally the cheapest printers available. They 'scorch' the printed characters on to specially sensitive paper. However, the sensitive paper is extremely expensive and cannot produce carbon copies. so we do not recommend thermal printers for the business of running a church.

Daisywheel printers

These exploit the idea of cutting the arms of an old-fashioned typewriter quite short and sticking them out from a small wheel as if they were spokes, then casting that wheel accurately in plastic or metal. When so cast, the spokes resemble the petals of a daisy, hence the term *'daisywheel'*.

As you tap the keyboard, a circuit in the printer lines up the corresponding petal with a little hammer which knocks it forward a few millimetres on to the ribbon and leaves an impression on the page. You may have seen modern electric typewriters working in this way. The print-head moves along the carriage as it prints, instead of the carriage moving as in older typewriters.

Print styles

Daisywheel printers often use typewriter components and technology. They give an excellent result on the printed page. Letters, manuscripts and masters suitable for photocopying or photo-reduction for parish magazines, all benefit from this typewriter quality or 'letter quality'. By changing the daisywheel you can also get a range of typefaces and print densities.

Typewriters

Some modern typewriters can be driven by a computer or can have a computer connection added when needed. It would be a short-sighted church that purchased a new typewriter lacking this facility.

Speeds

Daisywheel printers tend to be a bit noisy, but the latest are acceptable in an office. They tend to be slow by comparison with other computer printers, but still work at three times the speed of manual typewriting. There are two typical speed ranges, each associated with a price bracket.

For around £350–£400 you can have speeds of 15–20 characters per second from a printer that will print alternate lines of type backwards on the return stroke to save carriage-return time. If you do not mind waiting about five minutes to have a page of 600 words printed these will do everything you need apart from graphics. But we find that once people have these machines they tend to want a lot more speed. The higher speed daisywheel printers run at 40–50 characters per second and are designed for a heavy commercial load. It would not be worth the normal church paying over £1000 for one.

Matrix printers

The commonest printers for microcomputers, which we strongly recommend, replace the daisywheel with a printing-head loaded with a column of blunt needles. These are fired very rapidly by electromagnets at the carbon ribbon, to leave a neat pattern of dots composing each keyboard character. The more dots that make up each character, the better shaped and more solid it can look. So dot-matrix printers tend to cost more, as they offer more dots to fill the solid area that each letter occupies.

Character formation

The height of the column of dots varies from five to twenty or more dots and the number of times that column is fired across the width of a character varies from six to over sixty. Beware the very cheapest, the 5-dot high printers. They cannot form the descending tail of a 'p', 'q', 'y', etc., and make the text difficult to read by compressing a 'p' into the same height as an 'e'. These are not recommended for business use.

A minimum column of seven dots will give a truly descending 'p' and 'q'. After that, the more dots per column the better. Seven dots across the character gives very acceptable printing for collecting and retrieving information and storing it, for

27

preparing proofs or even for presenting accounts. However, seven is often considered unacceptable for correspondence, although we know people who use it for such. Eighteen or more dots across the letter give very nearly correspondence-quality printing.

Print speed and width

Speed typically starts at 100 characters per second, five to six times faster than the daisywheel printers, and goes up to 400 characters per second. The most cost-effective models are around 120–160 characters per second which will print out a 600-character A4 page in forty-five seconds. The advantages gained in faster printing speeds than daisywheels may not seem important to the casual reader but there is a big difference between waiting over five minutes or under one minute for a page full of print. For around £350–£400 very good dot-matrix printers can be bought that print 80-column (80-character) wide A4 paper at 160 characters per second (cps). Slower printers come a little cheaper.

Most of these printers have a bigger version that can print 132 columns wide, but we have not yet met a church application that needs more than an 80-column printer.

Reliability

The current generation of printers is very reliable and the Mean Time Between Failures (MTBF) is often published. 4000 hours of use MTBF, or two years continuous use, is common. This means that you can probably risk buying your printer second-hand, as long as the supplying dealer will guarantee it for the first three months, during which time any damage caused by the previous owner should show up.

Quality of print

Great efforts are being made to bridge the gap between the draft, or 'report' quality printing of standard dot-matrix printers and the daisywheels. If your printer uses a print-head carrying a column of nine or more needles it may well offer a choice of 'near letter quality' (NLQ), running at slow speed, with each letter gone over twice by the print-head to produce, typically, a 9 × 18, or 18 × 18, array of dots.

If you have access to a photocopier, or typesetter, that can reduce ten characters per inch printing on A4 paper to A5 you may find that it needs a magnifying glass on the final result to tell the difference between text produced from a good near letter quality dot-matrix printer and that produced from a daisywheel. The best dot-matrix printers can print an 18 × 60 matrix at 60 cps; and yet are priced to suit an IBM PC. Many people would be happy with this quality for correspondence.

Ribbons

It will help running costs if your printer takes a ribbon cartridge compatible with an IBM or Triumph Adler or a well-known make of typewriter for which there is a well-established market with competitive suppliers. Try not to get locked into a private brand of ribbon cartridge.

Print sizes

Both of these printer types, daisywheel and matrix, can offer several print sizes: nearly always 10 characters per inch (cpi), 12 cpi, and around 15–17.5 cpi. The best also offer proportional spacing, in which a lower-case i takes up one-third of the space of a lower-case m. The letters associated with proportional spacing are usually of the same dimensions as those used on the 10 cpi print-wheel.

On the daisywheels, the print size and style are changed by swapping over wheels and selecting a new print-switch position. The matrix printers are more frequently set to the different sizes by commands from the control console, or by a software program. Many matrix printers can handle graphics as well as a wide variety of type founts.

Ink-jet printers

Ink-jet printers are more expensive than matrix printers. We mention them because at time of going to press their price is falling fast to the point where they may be cheaper than a matrix plus a daisywheel. Ink is drawn from a small reservoir in such a way that very minute droplets are fired at the paper by an electronic gun, which aims them just as the gun in a television screen aims its beam of electrons. The printer is silent, the print outline is excellent and the system is fast. But they cannot do carbon copies, and their reliability is still unproven.

Paper-feeding

Friction

This is the simplest form of paper-feed and universally available, the friction roller merely feeding paper through as it rotates. In particular this lets you feed individual sheets of letter-heading by hand with or without carbon copies, exactly as on a typewriter. Its disadvantage is that it tends to let the continuous feed paper so often used with computers slip sideways and get out of alignment.

Pinwheels

To overcome this disadvantage, many printers have two pinwheels located at either end of the platen (roller). This allows one particular width of stationery with standard holes punched along the edges, usually mounted on ½" perforated margins, to be pulled through the computer by the studs of the pinwheel engaging in the holes of the margins. This pinwheel-feed system is, however, usually not suitable for A4 paper and so not a help for church work.

Tractor-fed paper

Tractors, which usually clip on to printers, cost less than £100. They carry a pair of miniature caterpillar tracks with studs on them that can be adjusted to any width of punched-edge paper. The friction feed is then disengaged, and the tractor-feed presents the paper to the printer. We consider it more important to have a second-hand printer with tractor-feed than to have a new printer without a tractor.

Bottom or centre feed

Most self-adhesive labels tend to unpeel automatically inside the printer if they are fed through the usual path, from the back,

The Epson RX 80 F/T computer printer with tractor feed

underneath and round up through the front of the platen. Trying to extract the last pieces of adhesive label from the 'innards' of a printer is a sad task. Many printers have a slot underneath, through which you can feed continuous stationery from a stack below, in particular self-adhesive labels. Always use this for the labels unless they are of the highest quality and guaranteed for feeding round a platen. This requires a printer-stand with a slot in the same place. And once you have this, you may prefer to feed all your tractor-fed stationery up the centre slot to simplify the paper path.

Cut-sheet feeders

Letter-heading is expensive and needs careful treatment. You can usually feed this through your printer a sheet at a time. But it does mean that someone must be continuously in attendance. To produce a headed letter to the whole parish you will need a cut-sheet feeder or continuous headed stationery, but this can be expensive. A typical sheet-feeder holds 200 sheets of letter-head which it feeds automatically to the printer. Many printers cannot be equipped with this accessory later so if you might need one, check before you buy.

Plugs

Computers feed their signals to printers from different sorts of plugs. Make sure that you choose a printer plug that matches the computer plug.

The types of plugs are:

- *Parallel* (also called Centronics): Very common and much the easiest for a learner to use. The cable is usually a flat ribbon.

- *Serial* (or RS232): Slightly less common, sometimes at an extra price, but able to send and receive more than just a printer. Usually a round cable.

- *Other private* printer cable systems. Not recommended.

You will find the Centronics the easiest to start with, and the RS232 the most versatile, if you do not mind spending time setting it up. For this reason it is essential that you get the shop to make the printer work for you before you take it home.

Where to buy

If you have someone who can help set it up, or you are fairly confident that you can master the instruction manuals, do not hesitate to buy your printer from the cheapest discount house. But if you may need a bit of help, buy from a friendly local dealer.

What you need

Ask yourself:

- Do you need a correspondence quality printer? Or will draft quality or near letter quality suffice?

- If you do need letter quality, do you need a complete printer just for this purpose? Could you not plug into a modern typewriter when necessary?

- Do you need to cut stencils? Printing stencils by matrix is tricky. Daisywheels suit stencil-cutting best.

- If you need letter quality, can you manage with about 15–20 characters per second printing speeds? It is much faster than manual typing, but does seem slow if you are producing 600 labels.

- If you are not tied to true letter quality, or can accept near letter-quality printing, you can use matrix printers, which are far faster.

Our recommendation is that you buy an 80-column dot-matrix printer with a Centronics plug and tractor-feed.

7

Floppy disks: a good read

Tape

How you store information dictates the cost of your microcomputer. In Chapter 2 we described how the signals sent when you tap a computer key can be captured and stored on the equivalent of a tape-recorder. Indeed the smallest, humblest home computers do use a C90 cassette-recorder tape to hold the electrical pulses which either tell the computer what to do, called *programs*, or record what you have done on the computer in *data files*. And indeed nearly all computer games sold in shops come on cassette tapes.

For someone running a small office, however, cassette tape has disadvantages. Each program tends to have to be restricted to the size of the computer's memory. Otherwise it is very complicated to add new information to the middle of a file stored on a tape. Cassette tape is, however, a good straightforward way of getting a program into a small home computer.

Disks

A better device, called a *floppy disk*, is now the key to business microcomputing. This is a plastic disk about the size of a 45 rpm record but thinner and flexible, with a smooth surface covered with the same brown oxide that you see on the surface of cassette tape. Instead of grooves, the surface is covered with concentric magnetized circles that store information. Each of

Floppy disks (5¼"), single-sided and double-sided

these circles is divided into short, equal lengths laid out in sectors.

The fixed recording-head we find in a tape-recorder is remounted to be able to move from the outside track to the inside track very accurately and swiftly. During any one slow rotation of the disk, the recording-head could pick up any sector on any track. When the disk is turning swiftly, the recording-head will pick up that sector almost as quickly as it reaches the correct track. Two outer tracks are usually reserved for a directory which tells the recording-head where the first piece of information it seeks is stored on the disk.

The head touches the floppy disk, just as the head touches the tape on a C90 cassette, so there are limits to the speed at which the disk can rotate and the head can move. The performance is impressive compared with a tape-recorder. A floppy disk can find any new piece of information in about 350 thousandths of a second.

Disk size

Floppy disks may have the magnetic recording on one, or both sides. Some computers have a single read head which can read only one side of a disk, others have two, to read both sides. Floppy disks are 8″, 5¼″, 3½″, or 3″ in diameter. Of these, the commonest on microcomputers in 1985 was the 5¼″ disk adopted by IBM, and this seems likely to remain the commonest disk drive for some time to come.

There are some excellent computers, of which the Apricot is a fine example, that use smaller disks. But the majority of programs are on 5¼″ disks in the IBM format. If you are lucky enough to be able to afford a machine using this type of disk you will seldom have cause to regret it. If your budget cannot quite stretch to the IBM type, any of the reliable, nationally marketed disk drives are still going to be of immense use to you, not only for the speed of access which we have just described above, but because of the amount of data held and the way that new data is put in.

Capacities

The smallest floppy disks hold about 96,000 characters of data. A densely packed 5¼″ disk holds over 1.2 million characters. The methods of packing the tracks on to the disks and of packing the sectors within the tracks vary. We know of about 250 different ways of 'formatting' a floppy disk. Another reason for choosing a disk drive that emulates one of the well-known, mass-produced market leaders is to avoid being saddled with a rare brand of floppy 'format' that offers you little choice of software.

There are roughly 2000 characters to an average typescript A4 page. So you can divide the capacity of your disk in characters by 2000 to find roughly how many A4 pages of text that disk will theoretically hold. One of these slim 5¼″ disks, encased in its cardboard square protective cover, can carry as much information as twelve A4 files, each with fifty full A4 pages. This

ST. DEINIOL'S HAWARDEN LIBRARY

represents the contents of a half-full filing-cabinet drawer with the usual mix of short letters, memos, and out-of-date information that is updated by subsequent correspondence.

Selection

New information is filed on the disk into the next free 'sector'. That location is recorded in an index held on the first two tracks of the disk. This type of information storage is being used day in, day out by many millions of computer users and gives very reliable service in practical use. However a disk that is more than 80% full slows down noticeably as it hunts for more space to place further information. We therefore recommend that you never load a working disk more than 80% of its capacity, which probably means starting off by aiming to use at most 60%. The minimum grade of disk/drive to aim for is just over 360,000 characters, which we call 360K. This will certainly cover a church list of 600 households or 900 individuals. But you can manage with 180K disks in a church of 200 people or a 96K disk in a church of 100 people.

Cost

If your budget won't stretch to a disk machine, a simple tape-recorder will get you by. Many of the programs available through the Church Computer Users Group are on tape and designed for use with tape. But a disk drive is of so much practical help that most people who have not started off with one later find themselves saving up every penny until they can buy a disk drive to add on. This ends up more expensive than buying one in the first place, so we would put a disk drive as the next most important thing to buy after a printer – much more vital than buying a colour screen.

Home computers

There seem to be two types of church computers. The first is usually purchased by the minister privately and ranges from the smallest Sinclair ZX81 through the range of home computers: 'Spectrum', BBC, Acorn, Amstrad, and such like, with 40-column screens, with tape-recorder storage and a modest printer. As the experience of using computers successfully has grown within the churches, so these computers have grown into more extensive disk-based systems, often in the end costing £2000 or more. This is a substantial sum for a minister to place free of charge at the disposal of his church, and is a great loss to that church when the minister leaves.

Business computers

The second type starts with those people who have their own business computers on which they kindly undertake to keep particular records on behalf of the church. These are seldom less than 80-column twin-disk machines and have historically embraced the 'Apple', Sirius, Apricot and, more recently, the IBM PC and similar machines. These have been matched by those churches which have been able to afford professional administration and the appropriate support equipment. In the Church of England one would also expect to find these business-grade machines at diocesan level. They can cost from £1500 to £3500.

Budget

Most ministers just cannot contemplate privately spending the £1500 or so needed to purchase the upper-grade systems. They must proceed carefully, by getting to know about computers step by step, until over a few years perhaps all of £2000 will have been spent on a very extensive set-up, or maybe less than £700 will have been spent on all that is needed to give one bit of vital support to that particular ministry. By January 1986 the Amstrad

PCW 8256 single 3¼" disk drive computer complete with 90-column screen and printer at £399 plus VAT will have very nearly bridged this gap between home and business microcomputing. Amstrad has reduced the most expensive mechanical component, the disk drive, to only one side of one small 3" disk. This is enough for basic word processing and brings all the advantages we describe for disk systems to an entirely new price range and market. To keep the price down, the printer has been attached to its computer by a solidly connected cord, not plugged in. It is a remarkably good printer for the price, but it is part of the package so there is no choice of printer. The main snags of the system are, first, that you have to turn the disk round by hand in order to use the second side, which is unusual and inconvenient, and secondly, the lack of a second back-up disk drive (see below) creates as many difficulties as using a tape drive. The new Amstrad is a wonderful advance, but for home computing rather than business. But we predict that a version with twin double disk drives and interchangeable printer ports will appear on the market before long at a somewhat higher price. Such a machine may well prove the breakthrough in small business computers that many people are predicting.

Security

We recommend that a church should follow the business approach and buy an asset that will do a good job and last. We recommend that churches should purchase a twin-disk drive IBM, or its equivalent. Both drives should be built into the computer, not strung up to it with cables. Any computer owned by the church should be able to keep records securely. This can only be done conveniently if a second disk drive is installed which will let the user take an electronic 'copy', called a *back-up disk*, of the changes made to the files that day. Then if something awful happens to the working disk – like being accidentally placed on top of a ringing telephone or getting soaked with coffee – there will be last night's copy to go back to and retrieve all the vital information from.

Strictly speaking you should rotate six back-up copies; to-night's, last night's, the night before last's, the end of last week, end of last month and end of last year. And the last three of these should be kept in a separate building from the first three, in case of fire, flood or theft, preferably in the church safe. But outside well-managed commercial operations, few people impose this amount of self-discipline on their computing. We do suggest strongly, however, that at the very least you use the copying facilities of your computer to ensure that you never work off a master disk, only off its copy. And every time you change some data, before closing down at the end of the work, make sure that you at least copy the data back on to your back-up disk so that you have something in reserve if you acciden-tally erase your working data. Anything less would be quite unprofessional, equivalent to typing important business letters without retaining carbon copies.

Handling disks

Your computer manual will have detailed instructions of how to handle disks, load them into the computer, copy them and store them. Read these sections carefully. Handled properly, your disk should give you many many years of trouble-free use.

Single-disk drives

Is a twin-disk drive essential? You can in fact 'back up' your disk using a single-disk drive, and people who have upgraded from a cassette drive regularly do so. This is a tiresome job, however, involving copying a part of the working disk into memory, then inserting another disk in that drive to pick up that slice of data, then swapping disks to load another slice, swapping back and so on. Unless the disk is very small, or the data short, this is the reason why back-ups don't get done! This is why a church should never buy a single-disk computer!

Winchester disks

You may come across *Winchester* (also called *hard*) *disks*. These are a type of compact hard disk that is not removable. They are hermetically sealed in a steel case, and a hard Winchester disk of 5¼″ diameter will, depending on what type it is, hold on its surfaces between 10 million and 140 million characters of information. The smallest costs about £1200 above the cost of the twin floppy-disk computer.

With a Winchester, you get a much better performance than with a floppy disk of the same size. A Winchester disk can rotate at 3500 revolutions per minute with the recording heads floating on a thin film of gas above the disk surface. (Floppies turn at 350 rpm.) The time taken to find a piece of information can be between 80 and 30 thousandths of a second and the speed of reading information is 5 million characters per minute, whereas floppies read at ¼ million characters a minute.

The better grades of Winchester disk are wonderfully reliable, although they still *must* have their data regularly electronically copied for safety.

Knowing the speed and facilities of a Winchester disk we only hope that some church, somewhere, will some day be given such a computer as a gift, perhaps by a Christian businessman who is changing his model for a new one. But we have to say frankly that no one has put a case to us yet where one could justify the extra cost of buying a new hard-disk computer for running an average church.

What you need

We have seen that the program instructions for your computer and the results of what you have done on it need to be recorded magnetically. It is least expensive to hold these records on tape cassettes, but most people soon find these very inefficient for business purposes, although they are fine for games.

Keeping information on a disk will bring you the true advantages of computing, which really become apparent with

41

the amazing speed offered by a disk drive. This allows your computer to access any item of information from within many hundreds of pages of data in the twinkling of an eye. We recommend 5¼" disks in IBM format for preference. Accept one of the many alternatives if you are offered a particularly good deal.

The church should buy its own twin-disk computer so that records can be kept properly secure by easily making electronic copies of the up-to-date files on to a spare, or back-up, disk via the second disk drive.

8

Software: the heart of the matter

We have given a brief introduction into the workings of those parts of the computer that you can see; these are conventionally called the *hardware*. We now come to a much more important part of the computer that you cannot see, the *software*. The difference between hardware and software can be likened to the human body and mind. Software is the suite of instructions, or 'programs', that make your computer work. These programs are highly refined analyses of what you expect your computer to do in a given situation. It is quite normal to buy programs containing several hundred thousand characters of code. So much is needed to ensure not only that your presumed wishes are obeyed when you ask your computer to perform a task, but that even your expected errors are trapped and diverted to screen prompts requesting you to 'try again'. It is the sheer size of the modern, mass-produced, programs which you can now buy that prevents any one individual coming up with anything equivalent by his own pen. The best software is the product of a team effort.

It would be quite normal for a moderately sized business employing twenty people to use a suite of programs covering its buying, selling, stock-keeping and accountancy books, that would contain three million characters of code – equivalent to all the characters comprising the whole Bible. Pieces of this code are fed into the computer's memory either from tape, or perferably disk, to perform the task of work needed. As soon as that task is done, its results are recorded back, preferably on to disk, and the next task taken on board in memory.

Operating systems

How the program makes use of memory and how it gets information from and to the disk is handled by the computer's operating system. Prior to 1984 there were many private operating systems like those used by 'Tandy' and 'Apple'. Between 1982 and 1984 an operating system called CP/M became very widely used on 8-bit microcomputers and set an international standard. It is still available on smaller microcomputers and is much to be recommended.

During 1984 the IBM Personal Computer using an operating system called PC-DOS swept the business market to become the firm market leader. By mid-1985, thirty business microcomputer manufacturers had switched to making similar computers which we will call IBM 'workalikes' using a compatible system called MS-DOS. Software designed for these more advanced disk operating systems now dominates the market, with every important program available for MS-DOS or its equivalent.

Software and you

Remember that what you want to do and the results you want to get are more important than the machine you use. Your choice of computer is completely secondary to a far more important decision. *What software you need.* With the access to good software you get through MS-DOS you will usually find that someone has already thought about your problem and done their best to solve it. So beware the enthusiast who has dashed off a program he feels sure you will want, but is full of little unexpected snags and hitches called *bugs*. It takes experts a lot of time to write a program that is relatively free of bugs and proof against most errors by the operator. The large international software firms continually bring out revised versions based on the experience gained by thousands of users. We recommend that you avoid being a pioneer. Insist on meeting somebody who has used the program you intend to buy in circumstances that are close enough to yours. We hope that, as demand increases, Christian publishers and bookshops will branch out into selling 'approved' software.

What you see

What should you look for in software? Ask to see it demonstrated, either on a friend's machine or in a dealer's showroom. Look for the clarity of the screen layout. Does the information leap to your eye or is it a confusing mess? Turn down anything that leaves you confused. It will not get better with time.

How does the program let you decide what to do? Does it offer you a simple list of choices (a *menu*) in a clear and logical order? Are you prompted to make a clear and unambiguous response? If these points are largely true, the system may well be 'user friendly', which means clear and simply laid out, as opposed to 'unfriendly', which means obscure.

Handbooks

Now check the handbook. Reject promises of 'there will be one soon'. It never comes. Eschew a tattered typescript, as the manufacturer cannot be selling many if it is not printed! Reject bad and confusing English, but accept Americanisms, as some of the best handbooks come from the USA.

Some handbooks (or manuals) will drive you to distraction. They have no logical sequence, no index, and are written in an illiterate style. Refuse to buy them; insist only on a concise, clear manual that makes sense.

Note that the handbooks for the computer and the printer are part of the software provided with each. Examine these handbooks separately before you buy the computer and printer.

Finally, we freely admit that the differences between various makes of computer are not always that great. If price, delivery and specification look similar, choose the one with the better handbook.

Compatibility

Just as people work together well if they are compatible, so do programs. If you buy one program which, say, uses one function key to enter 'PRINT BOLD' and a second which uses another key for the same task, you will be confused which to use. So it pays to remain with the same program publisher ('Software House') as much as possible. He should use like keys for identical tasks.

What you need

The average church *needs* three main program suites:

Word Processing – see Chapter 9
Database – see Chapter 10
Spreadsheet – see Chapter 11

The church may also be able to use a range of specialist programs, including a special-effects printing program for posters and parish magazine and hymn sheets and accounting programs if you have endowments or trust funds. By mid-1985 there was more cheap church-orientated software in existence for the Sinclair 'Spectrum' than for any other 'home' grade microcomputer, but some was of doubtful quality.

Remember that your computer is useless without the right programs to run it. So you must first find the right sets of programs and handbooks, software, to do what you need for your own ministry, then choose a computer at a reasonable price to run them. Look out for offers of 'free' software with your computer; these may represent a substantial discount.

9

Processing words: easy does it

Words form an important part of any ministry. One of the great joys that a microcomputer brings is the ease with which words can be prepared and edited before printing, and the speed with which it prints.

There are four elements to typing words on a computer:

Word processing
Spelling check
Mailing list
Mailmerge

Sometimes these are sold as separate programs. Sometimes two, or all, are combined. Often you can find these programs offered 'free' with a computer.

Word processing

This is the most dramatic use: instead of typing straight on to a piece of paper, the word-processing program allows you to type letters first on to the screen and, with an 80-column screen and with one of the better programs, you will be able to see them laid out on the screen just as they would appear on paper. (A 40-column screen will display the words but not the true layout.) You can then insert text, delete text, alter spelling or punctuation, move and rearrange sentences and paragraphs, scrolling the screen up and down the text, until you are satisfied. There is no need to print out any text before it is perfect, unless you prefer to proofread from the printed page. Having composed your text, you can hold it pending on a floppy disk until you need it.

Word processing on a Ferranti personal computer

Spelling check

You may get a spelling-check dictionary of, say, 20,000 standard words and probably the space for 5000 more words peculiar to your own profession which you may add as a specialized dictionary as you go along. Words such as the name of your church, theological and parochial turns-of-phrase are the words that you will enter into the special dictionary, which will thereafter be recognized in subsequent spelling checks. The spelling checker highlights any word that it cannot match and asks you to add it to the dictionary, skip over it or modify it.

We are not suggesting for one moment that either you or any member of your church has difficulty in spelling! But even the best of us makes small typographical errors when using a typewriter. The burden of proofreading is immeasurably lessened with the aid of a spelling-checker program.

Mailing list

Many word-processing programs offer a mailing-list feature for printing self-adhesive labels, on which you can keep the names and addresses of several hundred parishioners and print address labels out selectively or in total. A mailing list is never as good as a proper database (see Chapter 10) but can be a very helpful start. Because the mailing list is stored magnetically on disk, it can be easily modified to keep it up to date.

Mailmerge

The best programs offer this link between the mailing list and your standard letters. You can prepare the standard letter so that instead of saying 'Dear Parishioner' you type in, say, 'Dear *'. Then the individual salutation that you prefer to use for each member is picked up in turn from the mailing list and inserted in place of the asterisk. Mailmerge allows you to print individually addressed letters, so you can use window envelopes. These are less expensive than standard envelopes plus sticky labels. They also automatically address the correct person: with sticky labels someone may accidentally put two letters in one envelope and you then get a mismatch between address labels and letters. The best mailmerge programs pick up information from a compatible database, as we shall see in Chapter 10.

Modified layouts and typestyles

Word-processing programs can usually instruct the computer's printer to change the size of typeface, make the typeface bold or underline it. Separate programs let you alter the style of print from a matrix printer to design interesting headlines, headings, covers to magazines and even posters. This sort of work would give great pleasure to an intelligent sixteen-year-old. It helps to produce an acceptable print face from a matrix printer if you print in large type on A4 and have that photo-reduced to A5.

Handbooks

Word-processing handbooks, in general, are good. John Vogler, a reporter on *PC Business World* calls Perfect Writer II's handbook 'the best handbook I have ever come across'.

'Free' software

Some computer makers offer 'free' software as a concealed discount; usually this includes a word-processing program. The manufacturer does not want complaints so he usually supplies internationally tested software which may not be the most popular program on the market but should be reliable and give you the features you need. At least it will work on his machine! And that solves one headache.

Uses

A lot of time has gone into producing reliable word-processing programs. They form one of the most used features available on microcomputers and you can get good value. Word processing is probably the easiest way to learn something of what your microcomputer can do for you, and to become familiar with its layout. A dealer should be prepared to install it in your office and give it a quick test before handing over. In that case we would expect you to produce your first successful word-processed letter the same afternoon.

One parish priest allows the secretary of the PCC to do the minutes on his word processor. (How much better it would be if the PCC owned the machine, and permission did not need to be given!) Another comments, 'The computer does not take the work off my secretary, but is a back-up if she falls ill'. Many use a word processor to compose the church magazine.

Word processing is therefore excellent for composing sermons and creative writing – especially for moving ideas around and inserting comments and references, and for the lovely clean copy that is printed out at the end. Those who have adopted it for the order of service are happy and would never change back. Word processing also simplifies the complex typing job of issuing a regular prayer diary.

Some ministries thrive on the minimum of correspondence. Others feel that a personal letter is an important aspect of outreach and contact. For them follow-up cards on birthdays, feast days, anniversaries of marriage and baptism, etc. are vital pastoral tools. For these the word-processing features of a microcomputer are the only way to maintain such a personal touch in these days of scarce resources and pressure on time.

What you need

You can pick up the elements of useful word processing in an afternoon, although you can go on learning for years. If you need to write to your parishioners to fulfil your ministry, this will justify buying a microcomputer. If your only need will be the parish magazine and composing sermons and talks, then a word-processing program will be invaluable, but may not justify a computer.

Look for an offer of 'free' word processing worth about £150 on a twin-disk business computer.

10

Filing systems: connecting people

People are the objects of a pastoral ministry. If your congregation is no more than twenty-five people, you can almost certainly remember all about each of them and you do not need a computer to help you. Some ministers find that they can remember 100 people with equal ease. Few of us can emulate this, we need some kind of card index to help remember even 100 names, addresses and personal details. For over 100 members, everyone needs some sort of record system. By 300 members those records have definitely become a problem.

If you type these records via a keyboard on to floppy disks, a microprocessor can analyse this mass of information and print it out in any way you select. This advanced filing system is called a *database*. A computer filing-system reduces many of the administrative problems faced by the medium-sized and larger church to manageable proportions and is the strongest reason for buying a computer.

You can reflect on your own personal ministry and think about the way you set up and use a filing system. One database saves keeping several different lists up to date. There is no need to keep a separate list of church officers from those taking the parish magazine or from those who are on the electoral roll. One single list can designate whether anybody on that list is, for instance, one or more of the following:

(a) A current church attender
(b) On a list for visiting
(c) On the electoral roll

(d) A member of the choir
(e) Takes the parish magazine
(f) A member of the 'nurture' Christian groups etc.
(g) A subscriber to planned giving

Several pastors like to keep records of their recent visits. The computer can scan for unvisited parishioners to highlight people who might have been inadvertently overlooked. Done manually, such a task is tedious.

Many churches already keep the sort of computer records that would let them print out quickly the names and addresses of, for example, all members who are old-age pensioners and who have birthdays in October. It would take hours of searching to get this information from a standard card index or from various membership lists. With the key information already stored in a database, the list could be printed out promptly and a birthday party for pensioners born in October could be organized with no extra trouble.

Small database programs are designed to fit entirely within a home computer's random access memory. These come on cassettes for the BBC, 'Spectrum', Atari, etc. They are great fun to learn with and will usually hold the details of a modest list. But they soon run out of capacity: a maximum of from 30 to 100 records is typical.

It is best to get all the records for any one database on to one disk. Then you can rely on finding any one detail from amongst the thousands. Church databases tend to grow as their usefulness pays off in a developing ministry. So aim for disks holding about 360,000 characters which will easily hold 500 names, perhaps up to 1000.

We believe that setting up and using a database will provide the flexible and adaptive key to relieving the administrative burden carried by so many parishes. In others it will overcome the administrative barrier to dynamic growth. For all it offers an opportunity for an extension of ministry in a wide variety of ways.

Data Protection Act

A database gives the user power to look through all the existing records and do research work in a few seconds which would formerly have taken days, probably weeks. Such power frightens some people dreadfully. To meet their fears the Data Protection Act has been passed.

The Churches negotiated with the Registrar of Data Protection in the summer of 1985 to get a common form of approval for church records. By 11 May 1986, the Act required all computer-kept records to have been registered. Each denomination has advice for its ministers on registration that suits its methods best. In the Church of England the PCC and the vicar may each have to register separately: in the PCC's name for covenants, and in the vicar's name for pastoral information.

Registration under the Act is vital and costs £22 for three years. You could legally keep unregistered a list of names and addresses only to be used for mailing. But if you once used that list to telephone one member to ask them a question, or to make a visit, you would break the law. If members of the church ask you if you are keeping computer records you can assure them that all is above board and that they enjoy the full protection of the Act, as well as of your own moral principles!

What does a database look like?

The whole computer screen is offered up ready for you to lay out just as if it were a blank index card. The maximum size of each card, or 'record' as it is called, will be set by the program you have bought, and typically it consists of up to 256 characters. Each line of an index card roughly corresponds to what we call a 'field' into which we divide a database 'record'. For instance, surname, Christian name, title, first address line, are four different 'fields'. The typical database will let you hold between 16 and 36 different fields on each record page.

There will be a maximum number of characters you can use in any one field. You have to ration yourself however, because the size for the entire record will not allow you to use all fields at full length. Some fields must be kept short.

Two examples of compressed and extended database screens are shown on pages 56 and 57.

From these examples you can see that creating and filling in a database is not particularly hard. You may well find a church member who can set it up for you if the minister lacks the time or inclination to master the handbook. But there is a need for the churches to be able to buy pre-set-up databases. We hope that standard church database record files will soon become commonplace.

Reports and lists

Notice in the illustrations on pages 56–7 the surname comes on the first line. That is the key item (field) in the database to which the other items, such as title (Mr, Mrs, etc.) or address refer. These other fields can be reported or omitted. But the key field, surname, will always be the basis of any report.

So you can look up people's *names* in any set of contexts such as:

All the management committee
All the men on the management committee
All the men on the management committee aged over 60
Plus details like addresses and telephone numbers as required

You can normally sort on several positive relationships between the name and the other fields (details) on the record (card) at once, as just shown. The better filing systems also let you sort by negative relationships: all people who take the parish magazine in a street who are *not* on the electoral roll – this can be very helpful for outreach – or all on the electoral roll who are *not* participating in planned giving.

If you need to consider your church by households, one trick is to buy a database that also allows a sort by serial numbers, preferably a five-figure number. Use the first two figures as a code for the streets and the last three to show the house numbers.

One database on sale already set up for churches, 'Kuber-nesis', as shown overleaf, reacts to the date you enter as you

St Hubert's, Great Puddlesham   19 Sep 85

NAME: FREDA JENKINS

ADDRESS: 44 The Grove   TEL: 22134
            Little Puddlesham
            UPPERTON   SEX: F
            UP10 5QW   AGE: 57 BORN: 19 Jan 28 Estd

DETAIL CODES: MRS CW PCC V2 HG3 ER COV

VISITS FREQ: 90 DAYS   VISIT DUE: 14 Nov 84
PAST VISITS: 25 Oct 82   20 Jan 83   16 Aug 84   *Overdue*

NOTES: Teaches Economics at Puddlesham School.
            Keen on new hymns!

OPERATION: (Pastoral password used for <<)

M=Modify addr,tel,age,sex,details N=Notes & visits display<< R=Rename
C=Change visits freq & notes<<   P=Print non-pastoral data   V=Visit made<<
I=Inspect another name   Q=Print with pastoral data<< A=Add new member
S=Sequential inspection   D=Delete member displayed   Return=Main Menu

Kubernesis pastoral/membership system

56

```
Christian names ...... Noel John .....      SURNAME ............ Blakethorpe .....
Title and initials ... Revd. N.J. ....      House name/number .. 114 ............
Road ................. Rotherford Road     District ........... Barners Green ...
County/Post town ..... Littlehampton       Postcode B25 2ZL Telephone 8264 3531
Couple addressing*Mr and Mrs Blakethorpe Family addressing*The Blakethorpe Family

            * ONLY ONE MEMBER PER HOUSEHOLD SHOULD HAVE A STARRED ENTRY

Occupation ........... Minister            Male/Female ........ Adult/Teen/Child A
Date of B.17/10/47 Baptised 17/12/47 Confirmed 13/09/52 Wedding 10/12/70
Single/Married M Name of Spouse Avril      Record number 99114/1
Number of children 3 Names of children Mary, James, Elizabeth Giving Covt
Other household None                       Next of kin  Wife at same address

CHURCH MEMBERSHIP Full Groups       Mens Committees   PCC Responsible posns Scout
Worshipping status                  Reg Sacramental status             Comm
EXTERNAL C offices      Diocn synod Jobs Gen Sec CPLS Electoral Roll    Res
Skills/interests Programming        Public office held Governor St Mary Sch
Date last visited   11/01/86 Class leader/visitor    Tom Smith

MAGAZINES No reqd*2                 Distributor Mary Jones Payment frequency Qtly
FOR ADVICE OR INFORMATION CONTACT CHURCH COMPUTER USERS GROUP TEL 021 743 2971
Disabled/infirm                     Sick Services provided Harvest Parcel year 2
Denomination CoE Belief AngCat
NOTES
```

A comprehensive database designed by the author, assisted by the Church Computer Users Group, using Perfect Filer II switch it on. It recalculates ages from 'presumed date of birth', and always displays up-to-the-minute ages. The age feature would let you automatically print out all those who are due for promotion from one youth group to the next, or to produce a follow-up list for possible confirmation candidates. 'Kubernesis' allows negative sorts. It also automatically checks if you are overdue on planned visits.

We emphasize the need for printed reports: It is easier for each member of the clergy and each group leader to work off an up-to-date list than the screen. They should hand back their previous list, with any alterations, in exchange for the latest. A mailing-label list is also a sort of report. A Christmas card list with 600 names on it can be completed in two hours instead of ten days.

Free complimentary copies of the church magazine could be issued for three months to every newcomer to the parish and followed up by the magazine distributor with a request for a subscription, or even by a personalized invitation from the church to the Family Service.

Lists can be very short: each parent and godparent involved with a single baptism, the families involved in a marriage, or those coming to live last month in the parish. Such lists can be followed up with one or more appropriate letters taking about a minute to produce. As one minister said to us of his database, 'For me, in a funny way, the computer helps me to know people better'.

Choosing the size

A database program may come 'free' with your computer, or may cost from £10 to £50 on a home computer and from £150 to £450 on a business microcomputer, depending on the maximum numbers of records and fields. Twenty-six fields is just about enough for most churches and forty is luxurious. On field size, 40 characters is often found enough for 'comments', and three lines of 35 characters for addresses. Consider the maximum number of records you could possibly keep at the end of five years. These might include the electoral roll, together with all children, all people associated with the church and any outreach contacts. Choose a system that will take all these records, with a good bit to spare for safety.

Other uses

All advertisers in the church magazine can be another database, all suppliers of goods and services to the church could be another, etc. Then you can address advertisers regularly with invoices or canvass suppliers for advertisements.

It is important to plan what each database will comprise, how it will grow and how you will use it. Arrange to build up your main church file in stages. Get each stage running well for a couple of months before going on to the next. Try to use lay people to keep the database up to date. Remember that it is very much up to you and the other church group leaders to keep passing notes to the computer team of the changes that you come across to keep the record up to date.

Selecting a system

Try to see what has been done in a nearby church. Use the same system if it suits you. You may find that those records are by households. Most ministers with home computers have been forced to record by households to save the memory space occupied by multiple addresses. We recommend a large enough computer system to allow *individuals* to be recorded on the database. The pastoral needs of a child in a household are so different from those of its parents that churches should record by individual wherever possible.

If you are short of people to help set up a database one short cut is to buy the 'Kubernesis' church records system (see Appendix IV). This is available on Tandy computers, which use the Tandy private operating system, and on Apricot computers which use MS-DOS but use 3½" disks that cost from three to five times the price of standard 5¼" disks. 'Kubernesis' recognizes the existence of households. You do not have to enter the same address repeatedly for each member of the same household. You need only print one envelope when mailing several members of the same household. But the maximum number of characters per record is relatively small and the program relies on a string of codes, rather than separate clear headings, as can be seen from the illustrations. The system was not available for IBM workalikes at the time of going to print.

Getting started

Many ministers find that the creativity of tailoring a blank database to their own ministry is stimulating as well as very cost effective, and decide to go ahead themselves.

Don't get carried away planning a massive database, recording every conceivable relationship. It will be hard work for someone to collect all the details and type them in. You need to keep any details already entered up to date. So start modestly, then build up gradually. Try to get the names and addresses and one or two vital key features typed in to start with. Then you will find how much work is involved in keeping this up to date and how much time can be spared for recording and updating further details. You have to think about how many people will have access to the computer. We suggest not less than two, in case one goes away; and not more than four, to keep reasonable control.

Data security

Because of the Data Protection Act you will only want to keep on the computer those comments you will happily show to the person referred to if they ask to see their record. This means that there will be very little in the 'remarks' column that needs password protection from a secretary. Keep off the database record any personal comments about performance such as 'a good leader'. Nevertheless items of a factual nature which may legally be held on the database, such as 'age' and 'marital status', can be sensitive issues. So the best security is a locked box for the database disks, while the active word-processing, poster design disks, etc., can be kept quite separately in reasonably open access with no more physical security than would be used for your duplicating-machine stencils.

Other uses

The database now lets you do all sorts of things that it would have been absurd to even think of doing before. The time and effort required would not have been worth the modest results. One advantage of the database is that individual, self-effacing, people do not get overlooked. There is less risk of only an 'in group', of people who know each other, running and participating in the church. Once the idea flourishes that any list, from a full alphabetical directory to the smallest house group, can be selected and printed in a few minutes, tasks which were impossible now become commonplace.

Lists of various church organizations, for the leaders concerned, always stay in step, and if each recipient hands back a manually corrected list, the next list that is issued to everyone will be up to date.

A database is also an excellent help to running a group of churches under one minister. Team ministers find a database gives each member of the team access to the progress made by the others. The churches and/or the ministers should each be set up as fields on the record.

Planning themes to hymns, tunes to hymns, sermons to texts, or lists of where and when sermons were used, are all easy database adaptations. The groups of people and subjects covered by prayer fellowship-meetings can be listed under each prayer team.

Lay involvement

Once you have decided on a database do get lay people involved. With regular notes from the minister on the twenty or so changes in the parish every month, church members can be relied upon to put the details into the computer. It would help if all people using the computer know how to print-out the routine parish lists when needed, and how to set up and run personalized letters. Many a housebound mother of small children would welcome such a task for an hour a week or a morning a month. Bear in mind too that many young people commonly express themselves in play and work through computers. You will find them enthusiastic and responsible helpers if encouraged to participate in this aspect of the church's work. So the computer can turn full circle and help to bring people into the church community.

What you need

Except in the very smallest congregations, a database is the essential piece of software that will normally justify a microcomputer for a church. The church should own its database and thus should buy the computer.

Try to think out the database in advance. Do work at it in sensible sections to get it running quickly in skeleton form, rather than to never get it finished. Involve lay people in running it, even in designing it. Get advice from the local Church Computer Users Group contact or pay for help from professional experts, like 'Kubernesis' (see Appendices III and IV).

Buy a database big enough to take all the people you would ever need to list – with a bit to spare – whose data files can be processed by your word-processing package and mailing list, otherwise sooner or later you will have to start all over again. Try to get the database offered 'free' with your computer. This represents a discount of around £150 on a twin-disk business computer.

11

Spreadsheets: sorting out finance

The spreadsheet does for figures what word processing does for words. Spreadsheets allow numbers to be manipulated in a manner that you will find positively exciting if numbers attract you, and that you will find exceedingly helpful if figures are merely a nuisance in your life.

To understand a spreadsheet, imagine a blank sheet of the ruled analysis paper which is used by book-keepers and accountants. This is normally covered with vertical and horizontal rulings. These allow columns of figures to be added up into a series of totals and sub-totals, such as the monthly income and expenditure of a church fund spread over a year. You can decide how many rows and columns of the spreadsheet you will need for any given task, from a minimum of one row in one column, a simple rectangular box, which we will call a 'cell', to a typical maximum of 255 lines, or rows, deep, by 52 columns wide. You can get smaller or larger spreadsheets depending on price. You can also combine several funds into one spreadsheet.

Book-keeping

Spreadsheet software is useful in planning the source and use of funds. It allows you to build up your own cash book, analysis book and budgets in either simple or very detailed form. For example, you may have fees coming in that need to be split: you can instruct the spreadsheet to divide this for you every time you enter the sum in the fees column. You may keep several

FAMILY BUDGET PROGRAM
Copyright, 1984, Perfect Software, Inc.

FAMILY BUDGET	JAN	FEB	MARCH	APRIL	MAY	JUNE	JULY	AUGUST	SEPT	OCT	NOV
FAMILY INCOME											
Wages of:											
David	750.00	750.00	750.00	770.00	770.00	770.00	770.00	770.00	770.00	770.00	770.00
Sally	534.00	534.00	534.00	534.00	534.00	534.00	534.00	583.00	583.00	583.00	583.00
Earnings from:											
Rented Property	100.00	100.00	100.00	100.00	100.00	100.00	100.00	100.00	100.00	100.00	100.00
Other	25.00	0	0	0	30.00	0	0	0	0	50.00	0
Total Income	1409.00	1384.00	1384.00	1404.00	1434.00	1404.00	1404.00	1453.00	1453.00	1503.00	1453.00
EXPENDITURES											
Fixed Expenses											
Car Mortgage	276.00	276.00	276.00	276.00	276.00	276.00	276.00	276.00	276.00	276.00	276.00
Rates	65.00	65.00	65.00	84.00	84.00	84.00	84.00	84.00	84.00	84.00	84.00
Water	9.00	9.00	9.00	12.00	12.00	12.00	12.00	12.00	12.00	12.00	12.00
Repayments	22.45	22.45	22.45	22.45	22.45	22.45					
Car:											
Car	5.96	5.96	5.96	5.96	5.96	5.96	5.96	5.96	5.96	5.96	
Home Contents	8.23	8.23	8.23	8.23	8.23	8.23	8.23	9.25	9.25	9.25	
Life Assurance	9.00	9.00	9.00	9.00	9.00	9.00	9.00	9.00	9.00	9.00	
Hire Purchase:											
Appliances	5.00	5.00	5.00	5.00	5.00	5.00	5.00	0	0	0	
Subtotal (Fixed Expenses)	400.64	400.64	400.64	422.64	422.64	422.64	400.19	396.21	396.21	396.21	.9%
Variable Expenses											
Electricity	25.00	25.00	25.00	25.00	25.00	25.00	25.00	25.00	25.00	25.00	25.
Gas	12.00	12.00	12.00	12.00	12.00	12.00	14.00	14.00	14.00	14.00	14.
Telephone	9.00	9.00	9.00	9.00	9.00	9.00	9.00	9.00	9.00	9.00	9.
Food	150.00	150.00	150.00	160.00	160.00	160.00	160.00	160.00	160.00	160.00	170.
Clothing	40.00	15.00	15.00	15.00	15.00	15.00	15.00	15.00	15.00	15.00	15.
Transport	30.00	30.00	30.00	30.00	30.00	30.00	30.00	30.00	30.00	30.00	30.
Furniture	200.00	0	0	0	0	0	0	0	0	0	150.
Entertainment	50.00	50.00	50.00	50.00	50.00	50.00	50.00	50.00	50.00	50.00	50.
Donations	2.00	2.00	2.00	2.00	2.00	2.00	2.00	2.00	2.00	2.00	2.
Subscriptions	6.00	6.00	6.00	6.00	6.00	6.00	6.00	6.00	6.00	6.00	6.
Miscellaneous	10.00	10.00	10.00	10.00	10.00	10.00	10.00	10.00	10.00	10.00	10.00
Subtotal (Variable Expenses)	534.00	309.00	309.00	369.00	319.00	319.00	321.00	321.00	321.00	321.00	631.00
TOTAL EXPENSES	934.64	709.64	709.64	791.64	741.64	741.64	721.19	717.21	717.21	717.21	1077.21
SAVINGS or DEFICIT	474.36	674.36	674.36	612.36	692.36	662.36	682.81	735.79	735.79	785.79	375.79
CUMULATIVE SAVINGS	474.36	1148.72	1823.08	2435.44	3127.80	3790.16	4472.97	5208.76	5944.55	6730.34	7106.13

Perfect Calc II spreadsheet printout

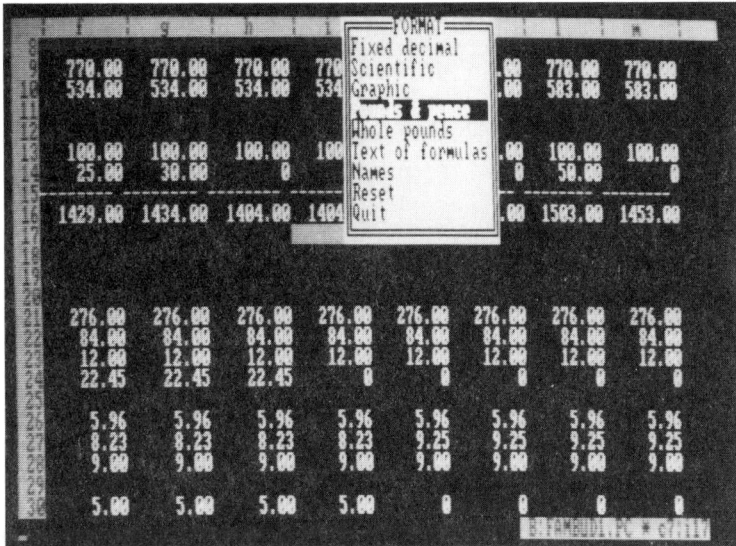

Perfect Calc II spreadsheet screen

funds in separate bank accounts to identify them. You may be able to consolidate all the balances on a spreadsheet and put them all into one fund on deposit account. Some churches could pay for a spreadsheet rapidly from this source alone. Do not use a spreadsheet program for pure accounting because it will lack the essential checks and security systems of accounting systems that force the print-out of daybooks and period-end balances.

Analysis

The higher priced spreadsheets let you describe each row and each column with a legend, even to embellish them with main headings, sub-headings, double rulings and sometimes footnotes. The cheapest spreadsheets automatically number the rows and letter the columns.

As you cast your eye down a column, or across a row, of figures on an ordinary analysis sheet you will think of yourself that 'this must be added to that', or 'this figure must be multiplied by another'. The spreadsheet can record each of these thoughts behind every box, or 'cell', over the whole spreadsheet. So a large array of calculations can be set up, one behind each cell formed by the rows and columns. Every sum that needs to be calculated has only to be defined once to be carried out accurately for you for evermore.

The spreadsheet program gives you this power to knit together, stitch by stitch, a complete fabric of calculations across a wide, deep page, sized A3 or larger. It will then reliably calculate those results time after time without making errors. This takes all the drudgery out of keeping simple books, splitting sums between different headings, adding rows, or columns of figures together, calculating percentages reliably, and doing these things repetitively and at a speed which even the most gifted mathematician could not hope to match.

Once you have a microcomputer, it would be foolish to neglect the potential help with book-keeping, budgeting and cash analysis which a good spreadsheet can offer, especially if it is offered 'free'.

How it works

A computer can in principle add two numbers in as little as one millionth of a second. But because the central processor also has to obtain the numbers from its memory, store the result afterwards, and clarify the mathematical instructions, most microcomputers can in fact add only several hundred numbers in a second.

The spreadsheet holds the relevant information in the computer's random access memory. The computer screen is then used to 'view' any part of the memory. Conventionally, viewing always starts off in the top left-hand corner of the spreadsheet, and by 'scrolling' the text appears to move both across the columns to the furthest right and/or down the rows to the very lowest.

As you change one figure, all the other related figures on the spreadsheet alter in step. So you can study the effects that different changes would have on your current budget, and examine the effect of, for example, 'giving' growing by 6% next year, of the heating bill going up by 9% next year, or of paid hire of the parish room growing by 8%.

Applications

It can be useful if more than one spreadsheet can be held in memory at one time so that cash can be allocated promptly to its appropriate paying-in and debit spreadsheets without undue delay.

It is also helpful if the spreadsheet is compatible with the database. Many databases do not offer much in the way of mathematical facilities. But several that lack mathematics can let you switch into the spreadsheet, do the mathematics and bring the result back into the database. This opens up the database to statistical analysis by those who are so inclined.

One limitation on designing a spreadsheet is how much of it can be got on to the printer. Scrolling the screen around a huge spreadsheet is fun, but it only gives transient information. As you will need a permanent record, try to design one to fit your printer, even if you have to switch it to the smaller optional print-out of 17½ characters per inch. This should give enough room to fit in a complete report of monthly inputs over a year, plus their titles. The normal A4 limit is about 66 rows deep. If your spreadsheet must spill over one A4 page, the better spreadsheets can print out overspill on subsequent sheets of paper which can then be Sellotaped together.

Points to look for

The best spreadsheets will allow you to scroll along the columns, say, from viewing January through to viewing December, without losing the row legends off the left-hand side of the screen. These should also allow you to 'freeze' the column titles into position as you scroll downwards so that you do not lose them and so can more easily keep your place.

Some spreadsheets let you split the screen into two or more 'windows', so that you can hold the totals, which would otherwise be off the screen at the bottom (for column totals) or beyond the right of the screen (for row totals), and see what the effect on any total is of work you do in the other half of the screen, which you hold focused on where you want to change a figure.

Some spreadsheets also let you display results in graphical form, such as bar charts or pie charts. Some of the cheaper spreadsheets expect you to fit all your numbers into standard sized boxes, or 'cells'; the more expensive allow you to save space by defining the width of any column.

Some programs allow you to enter alphabetical characters instead of numbers in the 'cells'. This lets you, for example, lay out complex tables giving analyses on non-financial matters such as for each week who will read each lesson, who will serve, greet the congregation, take the collection, ring the bells, etc. A similar spreadsheet can hold the names of all the people available for those tasks with the appropriate dates.

What you need

A spreadsheet is a useful tool for your computer. Carefully used, it can bring arithmetical certainty, speed and convenience to what may at present be some rather dull, book-keeping chores. This opens a further opportunity for lay people to help in the church. The money is more likely to be put in the right pocket every time, and added without error. So it is much easier to delegate the task of entering figures.

A 'free' spreadsheet is worth a discount of about £150 on a twin-disk business computer.

12

Programming: a temptation?

Some people find the sheer obedience of a computer fascinating.
To think through a problem, decide on a solution and record it
permanently on a machine that will go on 'thinking' your way
for as long as you wish is alluring. The very purity of
mathematical thought and the integrity of sound logic, add to
the triumph of writing a successful program. People possess
unexpected aptitudes for programming. Classicists and histor-
ians often make excellent programmers because they have
minds accustomed to disciplined thought.

Basic

A program is a set of instructions in binary arithmetic to
appropriate addresses in a computer, setting out the tasks you
wish it to perform and the conditions for doing them. Writing
these in binary arithmetic is tediously repetitive. So nowadays a
lot of these instructions have been bundled together into groups
which perform a particular, logical step. We showed earlier how
a thermostat carried out simple logical steps: *if, then, and* . . . .
Each of these words then becomes a codeword which is given to
the bundle of instructions that forms a logical step. These sets of
codewords are arranged so that strung together they form a
language. The best-known of these lists of codewords for
microcomputers forms the language known as Basic. It is easy to
learn and remarkably competent. More programs have been
written in Basic than in any other microcomputer language.

If you need to learn to program, learn Basic, either at evening classes or by reading a good book such as *Illustrating Basic* by Donald Alcock.

Dialects

Many of the home microcomputers come with a 'dialect' of Basic loaded into them. Just as a Geordie and a Cornishman both speak dialects of English, but might not always understand each other, so there are many 'dialects' of Basic. A program written in one will not necessarily work on a machine running another dialect. Yet there is a firm core of common usage throughout the Basic language family. Adjustments that have to be made between one dialect and another are usually easily mastered. Probably the most widely used dialect is M-Basic published by the Microsoft Corporation, USA, of which many similar versions are also available.

Time

A program normally takes between two and four times as long to write, test, make error free and put into working order as even experienced programmers calculate. Somehow the program that shines so clearly in your mind becomes impossible to put down reliably on paper! We all go through the same birth pains developing a program. Sadly, programming tends to be addictive, time consuming, and not very cost effective. None of this matters if you take up programming as a legitimate hobby, but your computer should be an aid to pastoral care, not a competitor for your time.

Higher-level languages

To save your valuable time, we particularly recommend that you buy computers provided complete with word-processing, database and spreadsheet programs. In these programs the idea of bundling commands together into logical steps has been taken a stage further into specialized fields. Word processing is itself a very superior language which allows you with one command to do very complicated things, like opening out a line of characters and inserting further characters in the middle. This would take a long string of program instructions in Basic. The same power of simplifying the instructions you give to your computer is buried behind a database program or a spreadsheet program.

So if you buy a computer that comes complete with word processing, a database and spreadsheet, you will find that this software brings with it the power to save many precious hours in programming your computer.

Many professional programmers admit that they write their programs using a word processor. It is so much easier than using the 'edit' facility in Basic. And some of the database programs, such as dBASE II and dBASE III are so powerful that thousands of programs have been written, using them as a language, saving up to 75% of the time normally used to write the same programs in Basic.

What you need

A lot of trouble has gone into making word processing, database and spreadsheet programs easy for the novice to use. Psychologists and professional communicators have vied with each other to make each company's program the most user friendly. And the opinions of many thousands of users have been fed back into continual improvement of the best programs.

In an ideal world somebody will already have written the program you need, and it will have been used successfully by people like you. As well as the commercially available church database program, 'Kubernesis' (see Appendix IV), there are several programs written for the BBC and 'Spectrum' home computers available through contacts with the Church Computer Users Group. The church does need good software with standard applications.

Programming can be fun. It can also become addictive. The three main working programs (word processing, database and spreadsheet) that we have recommended are in themselves very high-level languages which are very simple to use. We recommend you stay with them as far as possible. Nevertheless do buy a machine that comes with a good grade of Basic.

13

Buying a computer

So now you have reached a decision and are going to buy a computer. There is some money available, and a good offer in the local computer shop. *Stop!* This is where you need to remember *'Software first!'* – look back to Chapter 8.

The size of your system

Only after you have decided on software can you know how large a computer it will need. The most demanding program will be the database. The only regrets expressed to the author while preparing this book were by individual churches who could not now fit their needs on to the computer system. You feel sad as you try to fit the last of 210 names on to a database that will only take 200 records, or on to a disk that will only take 180 records.

Look back to chapter 10 on the database and fill in your answers to the needs of your database on the following points:

(a) Maximum number of records   = (   )
(b) Maximum number of fields per record = (   )
(c) Maximum size of largest field   = (   )
(d) Approximate number of characters, including the field titles, needed for a record   = (   )
(e) Allows 'negative sorts'
  (*not* a member of PCC etc.)?   Yes/No
(f) Able to sort using several fields at a time? 3–5–7–10/No
(g) Able to link in to mailing list?   Yes/No
(h) Able to link in to spreadsheet for analysis? Yes/No

(i) Probably for an 8-bit or 16-bit computer   8/16

(j) Probably for cassette or disk storage   C/D

(k) (i) Get help to find out how much storage this will need... K

(ii) This should be not more than 80% of disk capacity, therefore disk = ... K

Now you have a useful aid to carry while surveying the market. An intelligent and helpful dealer will be able to propose a suitable database and computer combination from these details.

Prices

As a very rough guide:

(1) For 30–100 records, you *can* use a cassette-based home computer.

(2) Up to 200 records, you should use a disk-based computer. (Possibly using 3″ disks) preferably running CP/M or MS-DOS Operating System.

(3) Up to 1000 records you must use a twin-disk business computer, CP/M or MS-DOS.

(4) Over 1000 records the program must have facilities to let you treat two disks as though they were one continuous record.

(5) Over 1500 records. You need a hard-disk computer.

Most parish databases will fall within the size range 100 minimum to 1000 maximum records, typically 200 to 600.

Price ranges for database programs are approximately:

(1)	£10–£50	With VAT
(2)	£20–£150	
(3,4)	£100–£250	Excl. VAT
(5)	£150–£450	

VAT

This brings up the vexed problem of VAT. As soon as a computer is aimed at businesses and the professions it is advertised as 'ex. VAT'. Businesses reclaim VAT, churches cannot and so have to pay the additional amount. In the rest of this chapter we have added VAT (assuming a rate of 15%), so that the prices are right for church treasurers.

VAT enhances the value of 'free' software, and of any discount that can be obtained on behalf of the churches. Never be afraid to ask for a discount. Several discounts are available through the inter-denominational Church Computer Users Group whose local contacts are listed in Appendix III.

Buying

The minister buys

The commonest case in all churches still is that the minister has to pay for computing. This is a dedicated act of vocation for, although the church may benefit greatly, the minister is making a loan free of charge to the church. Let us examine typical suitable systems that use tape or single-disk drive, starting with software. For addresses of suppliers, see Appendix IV.

The Masterfile database works well with the Tasword word processor. Prices include VAT, post, packing and discounts for churches:

For 'Spectrum Plus' (tape):

Tasword	£11.00	Word processor
TasMerge	£ 8.75	Mailing list
Masterfile with Masterprint	£17.50	Database
Omnicalc	£14.95	Spreadsheet
	£52.20	

For Amstrad 6128 (3″ disk):

Tasword (includes Mailmerge)	£15.95	Word processor
Masterfile	£19.95	Database
Mastercalc	£23.95	Spreadsheet
	£59.85	

For the BBC on tape in ROM:

    'Masterfile' database   £20.00

For the BBC on disk:

    Word processing, 'Wordwise Plus'   £36.80

    Database might be: { Betabase   £25.00

                     { Starbase   £86.25

We have mentioned these programs first and the following machines because they represent typical examples of what other ministers are already using.

In September 1985 prices were approximately:

Spectrum Plus:

complete with tape-recorder	£140.00
40-column monitor	£ 85.00
Software (say)	£ 52.50
Printer Epson RX80 F/T	£300.00
Printer cable	£ 17.00
	£594.50

Amstrad 6128:

with 1 × 3″ Disk Drive and 40-column green monitor	£300.00
Printer Epson RX80 F/T	£300.00
Printer cable	£ 17.00
Software (say)	£ 74.00
	£691.00

The BBC, cassette-recorder and 40-column screen:

BBC Micro with cassette-recorder	£355.35
40-column screen	£ 76.00
Word processing and database (say)	£ 50.00
Printer Epson RX80 F/T	£300.00
Printer cable	£ 17.00
	£798.35

76

The BBC microcomputer

BBC, single disk, and 80-column screen:

BBC Micro	£390.00
80-column screen	£ 85.00
CS4005 disk drive with power supply	£155.25
Wordwise Plus	£ 36.80
Betabase	£ 25.00
Printer Epson RX80 F/T	£300.00
Printer cable	£ 17.00
	£1,009.05

At the time of going to press, the author's recommendation in this class of single-disk drive computer system was:

Amstrad PCW 8256 8-bit, 256K RAM.
     Built in single disk 3" single-sided drive, 180K.
     Complete with CPM, GSX graphics, Basic.
     90-column × 32-line screen. With word-processing program.
     Printer with tractor, single sheet feed, pseudo NLQ.

          £488.00

Software: Very wide range of well-established
CP/M software available (say)   £200.00

          £688.00

Note that at the time of going to press there was no system for driving a daisywheel printer. CP/M programs on 3" disks for this computer may cost extra, hence our high software estimate.

As the months go by others will come on to the market. Read the reviews in *Personal Computer World* and similar magazines. Compare the new machines with those we have listed above for price and performance.

The church buys

We need to look at the whole problem of church computing afresh. Any computer is as much at the service of the church as the minister's car or the church organ. A computer is as important as a repair to the organ or to the church roof and compares favourably in cost.

There is every reason to believe that members generally will approve the idea of getting a computer. A minister, Fernley Simmonds, was given time off in 1983 to study this question and privately published his findings on six parishes spread both geographically and socially. He found that the majority of church members are either in favour of, or do not mind, their church using a computer. The only statistically measurable concern was over the security of records. A database disk locked in a cabinet cannot be read. This is a good reason for adopting the floppy disk computer.

The problems which were reported to the author were not with the body of the church but with its committees. It seems best if a working group of two or three is appointed by the management committee with the job of choosing a computer system and raising funds.

Churches have found that there is often a hitherto untapped fund of good will for a computer among their younger friends. Raising the money needed to buy a computer has not been as hard as expected. The right business grade microcomputer should last up to ten years if care is taken of it.

What to buy

We are concerned here with twin-disk systems. One microcomputer system has established itself as the dominating leader worldwide in the second half of the 1980s: the IBM PC with its PC-DOS operating system (or MS-DOS on workalike computers). The weight of users built up and software already developed for this type of computer prevent it becoming obsolete.

Computers designed for continuous business use rather than intermittent private use are more expensive. The business market is smaller than the private market, so the same economies of scale do not apply. The price range for a twin 5¼″ disk MS-DOS computer varies from about £1500, including VAT, without monitor or printer, to well over £3000. About thirty makes are available, with some coming and going each month. But the top ten manufacturers are well-established international companies. Of these, IBM holds the dominant position, with Apricot, on 3½″ disks, holding a very strong second place in the UK, but not so significant worldwide. For the UK the remaining nine leading 5¼″ 'workalike' manufacturers were, in alphabetical order: Commodore, Compaq, Ericsson, Ferranti, ITT, Olivetti, Sperry, Tandy and Zenith. Seek out someone offering one of these top machines. Look for as much good-grade software as possible included in the purchase price.

What you need

1. *Software*
   (a) Word processing; including Spelling
       Check, Mailing List, Mailmerge ⎫
   (b) Database large enough for all your ⎬ Compatible
       records ⎪
   (c) Spreadsheet ⎭
   (d) Good version of Basic
   (e) Good handbooks

2. *Hardware*
   (a) MS/DOS Operating System
   (b) Twin 5¼″ disks
   (c) Green or amber screen. 12″ size. Displaying 80 columns of
       letters either 24 or 25 rows deep. With brightness control
       on the front.
   (d) Processor with 126K RAM (256K if it does not add to the
       price)
   (e) At least one year's warranty. This is normally based on
       your returning the machine to the factory. *But an 'on-site
       warranty' is infinitely preferable and can be had.*
   (f) Good handbooks.

Which to buy

Having done many calculations to ensure that each specification
contains the basic essentials for a reliable system, you must
make your choice. The market is changing and developing
rapidly, so it is difficult to make specific recommendations:
However, at the time of going to press, a system by the British
firm, Ferranti, was being offered at a list price of £1552.50.

This price includes the following 'free' extras:

(a) Delivery to any address in the UK.
(b) 256K memory.
(c) One year's full 'on-site' warranty means that a service
    engineer comes to you if anything breaks down in the first
    year.

(d) The computer comes complete with a matching suite of software that fits our recommendations in Chapters 8, 9, 10 and 11:

BASIC
Perfect Writer II (UK):
Word Processing (with mailmerge and spelling checker)
Perfect Filer II (UK): Database
Perfect Calc II: Spreadsheet

} Compatible and tested as satisfactory for churches

(e) Parallel and serial ports. Built-in colour facilities. A joy-stick port for games.
(f) Lights on the *caps lock* and *numbers lock* keys.
(g) Access to the Ferranti systems' support telephone.

These items (a–g) would add up to a total of over £1000 extra on an IBM PC. The essential software represents a hidden discount of about £450, and the free on-site servicing another discount worth about £120.

Ferranti will supply churches which are members of the Church Computer Users Group at the following prices:

Ferranti 860 16-bit MS-DOS Computer, 256K RAM twin 360K drives £1041.90
    Monochrome monitor £ 96.60
    Centronics H80 printer 160/27 cps with feed tractor and NLQ £ 324.30
    (list price inc. VAT £1983.75)
    Church Price £1462.80

A wide range of software, printers, modems and add-on boards is also available to churches for the Ferranti 860 on the same advantageous terms.

An alternative buy

The Ferranti system will be very suitable where churches feel that they have the necessary skills or determination to install their own computer system. But there will be many churches

81

that cannot rely on the skills needed to set up a computer system. In that case you are again fortunate, as two Christians, Gareth and Sharon Morgan, have set up a Bristol-based consultancy for UK churches and have done a very professional job on the 'Kubernesis' software shown in Chapter 10. Not only is the program clear-cut and church-orientated but the nice conversational tone of the handbook is a tonic to read if you fear computers. A demonstration disk is available to run on a local Apricot or Tandy IV computer, and a support telephone is manned most days, and times, to help out those with queries. Further, the system is installed for you and left working.

So a suitable buy for the church which needs a little outside professional help, is 'Kubernesis':

(a) On a TANDY IVP Computer – using Tandy's private operating system, 64K = 2 disks and with a church
discount	£683.00
Epson LX80 NLQ printer	£280.00
Printer cable	£ 17.00
TOTAL hardware	£980.00

Software: also with Church discount:	
Kubernesis's Pastoral/Membership system	£180.00
Kubernesis Funds Handling System	£ 45.00
Scripsit	£ 47.00
TOTAL software	£272.00
Initial supplies, typically	£ 48.00
SUB-TOTAL	£1300.00
One day's consultancy assistance, typically	£ 100.00
TOTAL SYSTEM COST	£1400.00

(b) Generally as (a) above, but arranged for an Apricot PC Computer, MS-DOS, 2 = 3½" disks with monitor £3100.00

In both (a) and (b) above maintenance during the first year is by return to the factory via the nearest Tandy/Apricot shop. Maintenance insurance is available.

Buying secondhand

There is a growing market in secondhand microcomputers. A large number of companies, partnerships, farms and private individuals start off with a computer which is ideal for their first few years and then becomes too small for them. A lightly used computer from a reliable, well-known source would be ideal for a church. But do check up on the operating system. Try not to get stuck with an unusual one.

The risks are similar to buying a secondhand car. If you buy from a dealer you *must* get at least a 30-day warranty and see the machine demonstrated fully, with printer, before taking it away under your arm. If you buy from a friend or acquaintance try to make sure that the machine has been in a good condition previously. Advertisements in *Exchange and Mart* sometimes offer machines that are advertised as 'unused Christmas presents, still in their original wrapping'.

Make sure that the handbooks are all complete. A computer without its handbook and its software is completely useless. Try not to get stuck with too poor a screen and do make sure the computer actually drives the printer. The printer should have clear enough print and descending strokes on the letters 'p', 'g' and 'y'. Make sure that you do not pay too much; home-computer prices have been falling so fast that you may find that the proud owner asks a price which is more than the best up to date discount price new.

You might even find a free secondhand business computer! An appeal for a gift from a local businessman or woman may well be answered, because, until April 1984, a computer could be completely written off against profit in the first year. So it may be possible to receive a gift of a very respectable machine which is now being replaced by something even better.

The trouble with virtually all secondhand machines will be that they use an out-of-date operating system, unless they use CP/M when you can buy safely. If you come across a Tandy III, or Tandy IV, you can go to 'Kubernesis' for good, reliable software. There may be a few other similar exceptions where your local Church Computer Users Group will know of good software which has been developed for that particular model. But in general, buying a secondhand machine means not having MS-DOS and so being locked out of the mainstream developments which will be made by churches on business computers over the next few years.

Printers

When it comes to printers, the choice stays the same for both private and church purchase, because we do not recommend the typical home-computer printer.

Recommended choice:
Epson RX80 F/T Matrix printer, 100 characters per second, plus near letter quality with cable.   £300.00

Acceptable alternatives
Centronics GLP Matrix printer with tractor and cable. Draft speed 50 cps. NLQ 12 cps. One year's on-site warranty. 80 columns.
With church discount from Ferranti.   £208.45
Centronics H.80 160 cps matrix printer with 27 cps NLQ. (Ferranti)   £323.30

Possible compromise
Smith Corono Fasttext 80. Matrix 80 cps, 80 columns, no NLQ.   £212.75

Daisywheel printer
Juki 6100 18 cps   £400.00
(Or from Ferranti at church discount)   £342.70

The Church Computer Users Group can offer the names of dealers offering discounts to churches on printers.

Typewriter (church discount of 35%)
Brother CE61. With proportional spacing. Auto-centering, bold printing 10-12-15 pitch.   £345.85
Centronics interface for CE61   £109.25

Maintenance and running costs

A computer is like any other mechanical device: sooner or later it will need to be repaired. In the business world most people buy an annual Maintenance Contract to ensure that their computer will be repaired within (usually) eight hours of a fault developing. Most churches can afford to wait a bit longer than this, so need only pay for a repair engineer when needed. They can also usually afford the time to return the machine for repair when it is under guarantee in the first year.

The manufacturer will give you the name of someone who can repair your computer system locally. Get in touch with him and find out his typical charge for a half-day visit. Then, by the expiry of the guarantee, try to have a fund of about £200 available against the cost of a call-out and replacing spare parts. This will cover all the most likely failures, and the fund can be topped up again as it is expended. You would be unlucky to suffer one call-out per year. The only routine maintenance advised is to clean the disk heads monthly, using a cleaning pack costing about £15. You will also need a pack of 10 blank disks to make working copies of your programs and backup copies, cost £25; a spare printer ribbon, about £2–£5; and a box of continuous printer paper, about £14.

Conclusion

We have deliberately pointed to a standard which churches should aim for in computing. A twin 5¼" disk MS-DOS Computer with word processing, database, spreadsheet, Basic, 80-column screen and reasonable printer.

If you cannot afford, or do not need, this standard, you can still do useful things. You may simply want to get involved in Christian education, work with youth clubs, confirmation classes, and the younger children's groups. Much software for this type of work is written for the Sinclair 'Spectrum Plus' and it would be wrong to buy a twin-disk machine if this will be the primary emphasis.

14

Looking to the future

In the future computers will be used by churches as regularly as cars or typewriters. The first uses will be those covered by the earlier chapters of this book. One area of future growth is in communications. Already, using an electronic box called a *modem* which plugs between the computer and the telephone line, and costing perhaps £200, the computer can get in touch with other computers which are similarly plugged in. There are also experimental pages in the Post Office's Prestel communication system for church use set up from Colchester.

Computer-program swapping, even sermon swapping, may become commonplace over telephone lines. Church information that nowadays gets issued intermittently like the Bishop's diary or a diocesan directory could be kept up to date on disk at diocese level, available to access by computer. Much more use should be made of computers at diocesan level and deanery level in the Church of England. Documents like the electoral roll will one day be transmitted to the diocesan computer by telephone line.

As the use of microcomputers grows, it will become embarrassing to have non-computerized churches. Those without a computer, or access to one, will be administratively lost and backward. At this point we foresee one of the more successful parishes in a district being equipped with a hard-disk computer storing perhaps 10 or 20 million characters of information. Those churches in the district which cannot justify their own computers would then be equipped with a telephone terminal communication to the lead church computer at vastly reduced cost. In this way whole layers of computer networks will grow up within the churches, each according to the needs and traditions of its denomination.

One day it will be possible to gain access by computer telephone-link to the continually updated records of *Crockford* and to information on canon law, both of which in their published forms are constantly out of date.

We foresee tremendous advances in Christian computer games and Christian learning via computer. At present, few Christian computer games are good enough to stand repetition. Many make use of static slides for backgrounds which children tire of quickly.

Many tasks at a time

The less expensive microcomputers can only do one task at a time, say print or calculate. The best business microcomputers using MS-DOS can print out work while getting on with another task. So the printer may be sending out an annual appeal for stewardship, individually addressed to each member of the congregation, while you are composing a sermon.

If your computer programs support 'windowing', you can run both tasks, each through a separate, reserved area on the screen. It is just possible that you will notice either the printer or the screen hesitate slightly as it waits to use the computer. But the computer is so fast that these two tasks can be done together without noticeable inconvenience. Within the next few years the ability to do several tasks at a time will become very common.

New screen displays

80-column colour screens will drop in price. All business computers will be able to drive a good-grade colour screen for word processing. Colour word-processing is great fun on a good screen. Colour screens are very artistic, used with 'window' effects to separate each task better. 'Icons', or little symbols, that represent menu choices will gain greater use as computers reach ever less literate users. Much software for games is sold to children who can hardly read or write. As they grow up they will expect to be allowed to work with computers. Every one of us has a love of pictures, and pictures make a computer seem more friendly.

Speech

Voice input, to save keyboard input, has been 'around the corner' since 1953. One of the problems is that our own voices change if we are excited, or have a cold. It is quite a task to get the computer to recognize his master's voice through every change of inflexion.

Voice output will become very common. In the last few years great strides have been made, for example, in the voice instructions in car dashboards. And in the best programs you can choose the gender and tone of the speaker. Soon you will be able to specify a Churchill, a Mae West, or whatever, as your computer's chosen tone. The banal, flat and stilted computer voice of today will be a thing of the past.

Reading

Computers can be programmed to read ordinary typescript. And work is far advanced on reading handwriting. The larger memories available on 16-bit microcomputers have hardly been explored yet, let alone exploited. But there are mechanical problems in tracking printed text, and decoding handwriting makes great demands on memory and programming.

Outreach

Dedicated Christian programmers and Christian philanthropists and charities will combine to produce better Christian programs using new programming aids called 'graphics generators', which will provide all the facilities to make computer games, and become as freely available as databases and spreadsheets are today. Lively, mobile backgrounds and foregrounds and special effects will be available through advanced graphics generators using larger memories, so that each of us will be able to tell a Christian story as individually as if we were reading it aloud. The best will be published just as the best stories are printed today.

Costs

The real cost of 80-column screen business computers has dropped steadily over the years. There is not a lot of room for a further dramatic fall because the demands of users for support will still remain. There will be cyclical over-production which leads to spectacular cut-price promotions by direct mail houses and the large multiple retailers. This book is dedicated to help you evaluate their worth so that you can take a good opportunity when it is going.

People

On top of all this will come a change in people. Young ordinands coming into the ministry will demand computer facilities and expect to use them. Forward-looking churches will demand such ordinands. A church without an established database will seem fusty and dead. The younger laity will expect to use a computer to help in church work. Magazine printers will expect to print direct from the word-processing disk without asking for printed text.

Over to you

Most of these predictions already exist if only experimentally, in at least one of the denominations today. Tomorrow they will be commonplace.

The type of computer we have recommended foresees and can accommodate all of these developments. There is no need to delay. It will be best as soon as practicable to get two or three years' good, practical experience of using a computer to help manage the administration and outreach so that when these newer opportunities come along, the church concerned can give thanks that they were ready and waiting with their lamps trimmed.

APPENDIX I

Inland Revenue statement of practice on tax treatment of computers for ministers

(Reprinted with permission from Church Computer, *No. 10)*

Circular No. 1984/21

CHURCHES MAIN COMMITTEE

The Taxation of Ministers of Religion: Office Equipment

This circular, which has been issued with the consent of the Inland Revenue, is designed to give guidance to ministers of religion on relief which may be allowable for Income Tax purposes on expenditure incurred on the provision of modern technological equipment.

Relief is confined to expenditure which a minister has to incur on equipment which is being used to perform essential tasks arising from his normal ministerial duties e.g. the maintenance of parish records, accounts, etc. and, in the absence of which, he would have to undertake by traditional methods.

Paragraph 14(g) of Circular No.1978/21 includes, as expenditure incurred on secretarial assistance, the cost of repair or replacement of typewriters, filing cabinets etc. Expenditure of this nature, provided it satisfies the statutory conditions, may be allowed as a revenue expense under Section 194(3) (a) ICTA 1970. But, in strictness, the cost of providing a typewriter or filing cabinet is of a capital nature and falls to be considered under the capital allowance provisions of Section 47(1) Finance Act 1971. If a claim is made for capital allowances the same expenditure will not be available for relief under Section 194(3) (a). Expenditure on the provision of computers, photocopiers etc. is of a capital nature and falls to be considered under Section 47(1) Finance Act 1971.

Whether the expenditure is capital or revenue the test for allowability is very much the same. Capital allowances are due where expenditure is incurred on plant and machinery which is necessarily provided for use in the performance of the duties of the office. The test imposed is an objective one and one which has to be applied to the circumstances of individual cases.

But, as a general rule, where equipment is purchased to provide a more up to date and efficient method of performing a long standing duty, relief will normally be allowed. It follows that relief will normally be available where equipment is used in connection with the compilation of lists of church members, magazine subscribers, baptisms or other clerical work which had previously to be carried out by using for example, typewriters and filing cabinets.

The principles underlying Circular No. 1978/21 remain valid despite the passage of time.

APPENDIX II

List of computer applications in the parish of Greenside, Tyne & Wear

(By kind permission of the Rev. Stoker Wilson BSc)

1. *Maintenance of current wedding lists.* Weddings can take place at either of two churches, which means that there are two organists, vergers, etc., to be kept informed of the constantly changing information about forthcoming weddings. A list is maintained and periodically updated for circulation to all involved in church weddings.

2. *Sunday Service lists.* The planning of Sunday services and choice of hymns etc., is the prerogative of the Vicar. With up to five services on a Sunday, at up to three churches, I have to have the valued help of six to eight people each Sunday: organists, readers, preachers, etc. Each week a service list is produced from a pro-forma list and circulated to all involved in the coming Sunday services.

3. *Advance service planning.* In addition to (2) above, it is important to plan services well in advance. An initial list of four months' services is drafted with the aid of a pro-forma outline. This is circulated to all involved for comment and correction. The replies are then incorporated into the plan stored in disk, to produce the final four-month service plan.

4. *Hymn index.* Most hymn books have very inadequate indexes to assist in choice of hymns for services. I am currently using an indexing program to relate hymns from a range of books to certain 'keywords', for use in service preparation.

5. *Sunday Service notices.* A duplicated sheet is produced for each Sunday giving important announcements about church activities and prayer needs. This is produced from a pro-forma blank, saving considerable time on production.

6. *Preparation of baptism/godparent cards.* At times of baptisms we produce memorial cards for the parents and godparents. These are produced from standard commercial cards but the details need to be added for each family; perhaps four cards/family and five

families on a given Sunday. A short program accepts information about each family and prints out the cards using a daisywheel typewriter/printer.

7. *Baptism preparation leaflets.* We produce several leaflets for the guidance of parents and godparents who enquire about baptism of an infant. These need to be revised from time to time. The leaflets are stored on disk when first produced and are then available for easy revision when needed.

8. *Marriage preparation leaflets.* In a similar manner to (7) above, we store marriage preparation leaflets on file for revision as necessary.

9. *Agreement for the video-taping of a wedding service in church.* The diocese advises that a legal contract is drawn up between minister, bridal couple and operator before permission is given to allow a video-recording. A standard contract, following the official diocesan recommended form, is stored on disk. Local details are added when it is recalled and copies printed out for all the parties to sign.

10. *Baptism agreement letters.*From time to time parish clergy are asked to give approval for the baptism of a child in another parish. I store a standard letter, in which I state the conditions under which I will give my approval, for printing and use as necessary.

11. *Worship instructional leaflets.* The use of a large number of members of the congregation for reading lessons and leading intercessions in church services means that it is necessary to hold 'classes' for instruction from time to time. Appropriate instructional sheets to supplement the classes are produced and stored on disk for future revision and use.

12. *Committee agendas.* The vicar is responsible for planning and calling certain church meetings, e.g. the Parochial Church Council or the Standing Committee. Pro-forma letters and agendas are maintained on file and used with another file of names and addresses to print and address letters automatically to each committee member. Careful planning means that window envelopes can be used to save typing the envelopes with names and addresses of all the committee members.

13. *Parish magazine distribution.* We circulate over 500 parish magazines each month to individual homes, with the help of thirty-five voluntary distributors. The magazine list is constantly being changed with names being added and removed as people move

house, or die. The magazine is also seen as a main 'plank' in our policy of pastoral care and contact with baptism families. It serves as a link between themselves and the church at a time when it is not always easy to come to church with young children. The distribution of the magazine is maintained with the computer files. Revisions are made each month, and fresh lists printed for each distributor.

14. *Parish records.* We are building up a file of parish records which can be used for many different purposes, e.g. we can search the file for all senior citizens if we need to distribute charitable gifts. We can search the file for all children of a given age to print a visiting list as part of the post-baptism pastoral care. We can send out service or meeting invitations to specified groups of people.

15. *Parish electoral roll.* This is specific application of item (14) above. By law we must maintain a parish register of electors. This has to be revised for the annual meeting each year, and totally renewed every six years. At a renewal we must take reasonable steps to ensure that all persons on the old roll are informed that their name is being removed, and given a chance to re-apply. At the last renewal we had to circulate 660 named persons. The present roll has been reduced to some 250 persons, but represents a considerable work load, which the computer significantly reduces.

16. *Duplicating notices/handbills.* Good publicity is an important part of every parish. The dot-matrix printer, used with the computer, has a variety of typestyles and is used to produce very attractive duplicated handbills and notices.

17. *Service leaflets.* From time to time there is a need to produce service leaflets for special occasions, e.g. Harvest Festival, Carol Service, or Confirmation Service. The computer is used to compile and store these very effectively. It can also produce the stencils used to produce the actual service leaflet.

18. *Creative writing.* I have to produce copy for all sorts of different purposes: Parish Magazine, parish leaflets etc. The word-processing ability of the computer, with all the facilities it offers for editing and changing a document, means that it is much easier to write well and produce attractive copy. Since a large part of a minister's work is to do with teaching and dissemination of information, the use of a computer to help write well should not be underestimated.

19. *Vicar's monthly expenses.* Each month I submit a claim to the church treasurer for the reimbursement of expenses. This is handled by a short program which receives details of the various expenses, and prints out a claim form for the treasurer, according to the Church Commissioners' recommended design, as well as copy for myself.

20. *Vicar's discretionary account.* From time to time I am handed monies to be used at my discretion as Vicar of the parish. These sums are banked in a deposit account until needed and the administration of the account is made much easier by using a computer to help balance and analyse the account from time to time.

21. *Church fees account.* As Vicar I receive fees from a number of sources, principally from funerals and weddings. These fees have to be disbursed to organist, verger and PCC and myself. Accurate records are needed for the Inland Revenue, and also for the Church Commissioners who calculate salary levels on the basis of the figures supplied. Once again the clergy and PCC portion of these fees are banked; monthly transfers being made as necessary. The computer maintenance of these accounts is a great help.

APPENDIX III

Church Computer Users Group regional contacts

BIRMINGHAM. The Rev. Nigel Hardcastle. 021-743 2971
  12 Rotherfield Road, Garretts Green, Birmingham, B26 2SH

CANTERBURY/E. KENT. The Rev. Pat Goodsell. (030 381) 3168
  The Vicarage, Harringe Lane, Sellindge, Ashford, Kent, TN25 6HP

CHELMSFORD & NORTH LONDON. The Rev. Chris Bard. (0378) 72949
  The Vicarage, Epping Green, Epping, Essex, CM16 6PN

DERBYSHIRE. Mr Godfrey Hall. (0246) 851487
  91 St. Lawrence Road, North Wingfield, Chesterfield, Derbys, S42 5LJ

EAST ANGLIA. The Rev. J. S. Wood. (0473) 49222
  31 Preston Drive, Ipswich, Suffolk, IP1 6DS

HERTS & BEDS. Dr Robert Leggat. (0234) 67809
  Prestel Mailbox – 023467809
  1 Aldens Mead, Bedford, Beds, MK14 8JZ

NORTH EAST. The Rev. Stoker Wilson (091) 4138281
  Prestel Mailbox – 914138281
  St John's Vicarage, Greenside, Ryton, Tyne & Wear, NE40 4AA

NORTH WALES. The Rev. John Barden Davies. (0492 69) 507
  The Rectory, Llanbedr, Conway, Gwynedd, LL32 8UP

NORTH EAST. The Rev. Hugh Bonsey. (0744) 815158
  All Saints Vicarage, Waterdale Crescent, Sutton, St Helens, Merseyside.

NORTHERN IRELAND. The Ven. Jack Shearer. (0762) 332538
  Seagoe Rectory, 8 Upper Church Lane, Portadown, N. Ireland, BT63 5JE

PETERBOROUGH. Mr Kenneth Alvey. (0733) 263303
  89 Cleatham, Bretton, Peterborough, Cambs, PE3 6XG

SCOTLAND. The Rev. A. Ian Watt. (0577) 62271
Prestel Mailbox – 057762271
St Paul's Rectory, The Muirs, Kinross, Tayside, KY13 7AU

SHROPSHIRE & MID WALES. The Rev. Tony Lewis. (0691) 653652
34 Ferrers Road, Oswestry, Shropshire.

SOUTH WEST. The Rev. Roger Hoare. (0367) 20154
Prestel Mailbox – 036720154
The Vicarage, Coach Lane, Farringdon, Oxon, SN7 8AB

SOUTHERN. Mr Mark Jeffrey.
6 Warland Way, Corfe Mullen, Wimborne, Dorset, BH21 3NZ

THAMES VALLEY. The Rev. Brian Cowell. (0256) 722021
The Rectory, Up Nately, nr. Basingstoke, Hants, RG27 9PR

WAKEFIELD. The Rev. Kit Widdows. (0422) 54448
St Hilda's Church, Gibraltar Road, Halifax, W. Yorks, HX1 4HE

WEST KENT/S.E. LONDON. Mr Dennis Rump. 01-303 3957
11 Arcadian Avenue, Bexley, Kent, DA5 1JN

APPENDIX IV

Suppliers and addresses

'Brother' from: Office Equipment Selection Limited,
System 800 House,
Mylord Crescent,
Camperdown Industrial Estate,
Killingworth,
Newcastle Upon Tyne,
NE12 0UJ   091 268333

Ferranti from: Ferranti PC Sales,
Ferranti Computer Systems Limited,
Derker Street,
Oldham,
Lancs., OL1 3XF   061-624 9552

'Masterfile' from: Campbell Systems,
57 Traps Hill,
Loughton,
Essex, IG10 1TD   01-508 5058

'Kubernesis' from: Gareth Morgan Computer Services,
56 Devon Road,
Bristol, BS5 9AY   0272 559616

'Tasword' from: Tasman Software,
Springfield House,
Hyde Terrace,
Leeds, LS2 9LN   0532 438310

Consultant on church computer accounting systems:
Mr Richard Goddard,
RGS Computer Consultants,
Park Terrace,
Kingsland,
Leominster, HR6 9SQ   056 881577

APPENDIX V

Bibliography

Alcock, Donald, *Illustrating Basic*. Cambridge University Press, 1982.

Chandor, Anthony *et al*, eds., *The Penguin Dictionary of Computers*. Penguin, 1985.

Freeman, Richard, *Step by step Basic, for BBC Micro*. Lifelong Learning, 1983.

Hartnell, Tim, *Getting Started on your BBC Micro*. Futura, 1983.

Herbert, Frank, and Barnard, Max, *The Home Computer Handbook*. Gollancz, 1985.

Jackson, Peter, *Business Programming on your Spectrum Computer*. Phoenix, 1984.

Parr, E.A., *The Beginner's Guide to Microprocessors*. Newnes, 1982.

Parsons, Michael, *The Parish Computer*. Grove, 1984.

Thomas, Alan, *Further Programming for the BBC Micro*. Shiva, 1983.

Wilson, R.S., *Church Computer Directory*. CCUG, 1984.

————— *Computers in the Church*. CCUG, 1984.

APPENDIX VI

Glossary

Apricot   A popular make of business microcomputer.

ASCII   American Standard Code for Information Interchange.

Basic   A high-level programming language for developing programs in conversational mode depending on line numbering for sequencing.

BBC   A popular make of home computer.

Binary arithmetic   Arithmetic based on the numbers 0 and 1 only.

Bit   One of the two digits used in binary arithmetic.

Bugs   Unforeseen snags in a program.

Business computer   A microcomputer with at least the following features: twin double-sided floppy disk drives, an 80-column screen and a versatile printer.

Cell   The space in a spreadsheet formed by a column crossing a row.

Central processor   See **Microprocessor**.

Computer   An eletronic device to receive information, process it and supply specific results.

CP/M   An internationally used disk operating system.

Daisywheel   A printer that prints solid characters from a fount mounted on the many spokes of a small wheel.

Data files   Files of information created by the computer.

Database   A file that allows different requirements to take various information from the file, or update it, without affecting its design or content.

Disk   See **Floppy disk**.

Disk drives   The mechanical devices which spin, read and write to the floppy disks.

Disk operating system   The program which controls the flow of information between the floppy disks and the memory.

Field   The smallest complete slice of information in a database record.

Floppy disk   A thin, round, plastic sheet coated with fine oxide which can store information needed by a computer.

Function key   A part of the keyboard used by some programs to enter frequently needed commands.

Hard disk   See **Winchester disk**.

Hardware   All the physical units which make up a computer system.

Home computer   An inexpensive microcomputer usually with a 40-character screen, tape or single-disk input, a limited keyboard and restricted printer.

IBM   The most widely used make of business microcomputer.

Icons   Stylized pictures to designate tasks available to the computer.

Information technology   The art of handling and processing information electronically.

'K'   1000; also 1024 units of memory.

Keyboard   A set of keys arranged like a typewriter keyboard but with additional keys and legends, to work a computer.

Magnetic storage   Both the memory and the disk or tape storage.

Matrix printer   A printer that prints characters made up of many dots.

Memory   The immediate-access information store in a computer.

Menu   A list of choices offered via a computer screen to the operator.

Microcomputer   A small computer relying on a mass-produced central processor.

Microprocessor   The array of circuits photo-etched on a chip of silicon that will perform the logical steps instructed by a program.

Modem   An electronic box that will connect the serial (RS232) port of a microcomputer to the telephone system to send and receive.

Monitor   A television-like screen that displays information flowing to and from a computer.

MS-DOS   The most widely used disk operating system.

Operating system   See **Disk operating system.**

PC   Personal computer.

PC-DOS   The IBM version of MS-DOS.

Printer   A small machine for recording on paper the results from a computer.

Program   All the sets of logical steps by which a computer will solve a set of problems.

Programmer   A person who writes programs.

RAM   See **Random access memory.**

Random access memory   Information storage, any part of which can be reached instantly by the microprocessor to read or write.

Read only memory   Information storage that cannot be altered by using the computer.

Record   The building brick of information from which the database is constructed. For example, all the information on one church member should form one record.

ROM   See **Read only memory**.

Scroll   To make the text appear to move down or across the screen.

Sectors   Convenient divisions in the tracks of a floppy disk.

Sinclair 'Spectrum'   A popular make of home computer.

Software   Programs and their handbooks that can be used on that computer.

'Spectrum'   See **Sinclair 'Spectrum'**.

Spreadsheet   A program for manipulating tables of figures.

Tape   The magnetic tape contained in a C90 type cassette.

Tracks   The magnetic circles on a floppy disk in which information is stored.

Tractor   An attachment to a printer which drags continuous paper through it by gripping punched holes along each edge.

Winchester disk   An hermetically sealed metal disk whose head does not touch the disk, usually holding 10 million+ characters. Faster than a floppy disk.

Windows   Partitions of the computer screen, showing details from separate sources in the different partitions.

Word processor   A computer system for creating and editing text.

The Church Computer Users Group

The Church Computer Users Group is an independent, interdenominational organization which offers support to those involved in using computers and their associated technology for the glory of God and the work of the church. Any member of any church who is interested in using computers for this purpose is eligible for membership. The cost of membership is £5.00 per annum, for which members receive a copy of the Church Computer Directory listing all known available church software, and also three copies per year of the magazine 'Church Computer'. A wide range of activities is organized on a regional basis, with a particular emphasis on the exchange of information, advice and programs. Discounts have also been negotiated with suppliers for the benefit of members. An application form is printed on the opposite page for those interested in joining the CCUG.

CANCELLED

HAWARDE

LIBRA

Appendix

MEMBERSHIP APPLICATION FORM

TO: The Rev. Graham Spicer,   OFFICE USE ONLY
    Membership Secretary,   Membership Number
    Church Computer Users Group,
    30 The Crescent,   Year ending
    SOLIHULL,
    West Midlands,   Verified by
    B91 1JR

I apply for membership of the Church Computer Users Group and enclose my initial subscription of £5.00, for which you will send me membership documents and appropriate copies of 'Church Computer' magazine and the Church Computer Directory.

SURNAME ....

CHRISTIAN NAME ....

TITLE AND INITIALS ....

ADDRESS ....

....

POSTAL TOWN/CITY ....

COUNTY ....

POSTCODE ....

PHONE ....

PARISH/CHURCH ....

DENOMINATION ....

EXISTING/PROPOSED COMPUTER ....